ROUNDING
the CURVES

by ROXY CROSS

Edited by Lil Barcaski and Linda Hinkle

Published by: GWN Publishing
www.GWNPublishing.com

Cover Design: Kristina Conatser Captured by KC Design

Cover Photo Credit: Josh Cross, founder of DEFI Now and the Coin Academy, YouTube.com/c/DeFiNOW

ISBN: 978-1-959608-17-2
E-Book ISBN: 978-1-959608-18-9

DEDICATION

This book is dedicated to Jason Andrew Cross, whose coming into the world made me a mother for the first time. Motherhood, my greatest joy!

This bright inquisitive child grew into a man who has lived through extreme trauma, the kind of which flattens people unprepared. And to this day he is still curious, appreciating nature, while working to improve himself and his life.

I hope he tells his stories someday as they are something else… true and unbelievable. Until then, these are my stories, much of which is being Jason's mom.

May our stories inspire you to look at your life, searching for how it could be better, to motivate you to get after it!

Grace and peace.

CONTENTS

INTRODUCTION

Don't be afraid to cry. It will free your mind of sorrowful thoughts.
— HOPI PROVERB

I love it when a long-term plan comes together! I have been a professional writer, which means getting paid, since 1986. The various genres I have explored through the years, is an extensive list. I have written research papers, a national magazine column, a weekly newspaper column, kid's stories, over 1,000 web pages, award-winning commercials, greeting card sentiments and that is the tip of the iceberg. My blog, "To a Peaceable Life," has been going on WordPress since 2005, and is more active at some times than it has been lately. What has always been in the back of my mind is to write a book, even though I was not sure what kind of book. **CREATIVE**.

Fiction writing has not been my 'go to' other than writing children's books. Then, about a year ago, I attended a writing workshop from an east coast publisher visiting Salt Lake City. That's where I live.

We were asked to write 1,500 words on something important to us, in the 4-hour workshop.

The other participants wrote about non-profits they meant to create to resolve challenges in their communities.

I wrote about the lack of character strengthening I saw around me. Those around me were not learning how to build strong character behaviors and with the way things seemed to be going in the world, my concern was most people would not be able to find the way through hard times. **EMPATHY.**

My 1500-word piece told a couple of stories, shared in this book about resilience and getting through hard times. When I finished reading, one participant said, "I don't have children. I don't want children, but I want to read your book!"

Others commented and agreed and then the class instructor got my attention.

Lil said she did not believe anyone had written a great book on being resilient and I should write it. She said she was not sure if resiliency could be taught. I felt it was worth the effort to help people get through the tough times in life. I thought of a compliment my youngest daughter had given me a few years earlier.

"You are the most resilient person I know," my daughter said. It won't surprise you as my first thought was, 'well I'm tired of having to be resilient! Could I not have a simpler, kinder life by now?'

If this was the kind of response I would get from successful entrepreneurs, perhaps my now publisher, Lil, was right. Maybe it was time I started working on telling the stories of how I navigated through my crazy life, and what I learned along the way. I hoped it would help others.

I was raised by a Missouri, "Show Me" state, mom who grew up during the Great Depression. That and the fact I was married to a "gypsy," which lifestyle, though never boring, kept us poor for 23 years, means I have learned how to be resourceful and to make the best of what I had to work with daily.

My young family lived for years in circumstances without running water, using an outhouse, cooking over a fire, or a coal or wood burning stove or even a camp stove. I have cleaned the week's dirty washing in the river, discovering I appreciated my ancestors, and their hard lifestyles. It was such physically hard work; I could not move the next day! My whole body felt beaten!

Our family of five kids, at one time, camped from May to October in two adjacent tents on the Little Bear River, in northern Utah. Ten-year-old Jason, Trevor who was seven, David was five, Stephan was three and Alex was barely one. Their father, John, left for work, every morning to build homes, and did not return till well after dark. Without a phone or vehicle, the kids and I were miles from civilization, on a river, in Utah's mountains.

Our campsite was clean. We knew to keep our garbage away from our camp and out of reach of any wandering animals. People took an interest in us while we were living in the canyon. We were in church on time, clean and nicely dressed on Sunday.

Locals offered to teach me how to cook Dutch oven meals which was such a great skill! They taught me to cook various types of fish on a board sitting diagonal at the edge of the fire. It did not take long to give up trying to boil pasta or rice, as the altitude would never let the fire get hot enough to boil. It was so weird for this Chicago girl. I watched our food dissolve into a lifeless pasty mess at my pointless attempts!

Spending time with locals, we learned which plants were edible and what herbs grew in that canyon. By we, I mean my son, Trevor and I! He was the kid who loved learning about these things! **ADAPTABLE**.

My midwife, who helped me with Alex's birth, taught me about all kinds of herbs during my pregnancy with him. Before she got a hold of me, I knew nothing about herbs nor their healing powers. I jumped on this topic after a crazy experience which tested my view of myself as a mother. That story ends this book.

One of the advantages of being older now, is I remember things which are hard or impossible to find on the interweb now. That is what I call it when people misuse it. The interweb. You should be able to log on to the interweb to search anything you need to know, like how to take care of a child in need.

- What is a natural remedy for puncture wounds?
- What herb stops skin from burning?
- Which herbs are skin healers?
- Is there an herb you can use to stop bleeding?

Go ahead and look any of these up and if you can find it, send me the URL!

My point here is you may not be able to 'fact check' me on this, as information is controlled so well now. You will just have to decide if I am telling the truth or decided to lie to you after baring my heart and soul in the next 24 chapters! My wealth of accumulated knowledge kept my kids healthy and well while growing up. **GRATITUDE**.

You have been trained for decades, even generations to be afraid of tetanus, for instance. It is nasty, I understand that, however the most probable location to get tetanus, is in a horse corral, directly from horse manure. Yep, you heard right. When was the last time you were in a horse corral, messing about with horse manure?

Also, the virus in the horse manure, yep, let me repeat that, has to enter the body via a puncture wound so it does not get any air. Anaerobic. So, the puncture wound, gets horse manure/tetanus virus inside. I learned this after dealing with the head of St Joseph's Hospital in Omaha Nebraska about 38 years ago. That story is saved for another book.

This book is the first in a series. The intent is to share real stories happening in real lives, and the tools learned along the way. This way, if it resonates with you, you can find tools you can use, inspiration and peace in your own life. Occasionally, at the end of a paragraph you will see a character trait, all caps and bold. This is to recognize at least one character trait being developed in that story, if not more than one. **CALM**.

In a world where I do not know where you are going to learn solid character traits anywhere else, with busy families and churches with other focuses, I hope you will see them here, then consider your own life and how you can strengthen your own character. It is only by strengthening your character traits you will be able to navigate the challenging times of your life with resiliency, building what you need within yourself to be a wise human, able to withstand whatever is coming. I believe in you.

Grab a glass of water, a box of tissues, and let's jump in!

Mazel tov!

Note: Character and personality traits are in all caps at the end of many paragraphs to connect a main trait with that part of the story. You will notice how often traits handle getting through life's traumas and challenges. **INSPIRE**.

CHAPTER 1

GEEZ

GROWTH HURTS
Stacey Allen

Like the exit from a cocoon
Before a beautiful butterfly can soar...
It's an excruciating process
When through the pain it tore
Obedience over sacrifice
A convenient calling...no such thing...
How many generations will you let us impact?
What will our purpose bring?
So, I invite you into my weakness
Because I want there to be a void when I die...
Hurting SO much from the growth
Getting back up with every failed try
A void because I did something on this earth
A purpose to impart...
The "sweet stuff" that makes a difference
The atmosphere that changed a heart
Don't let us steal from others

Because selfishness lead the way…
Growth hurts…it's uncomfortable
Let us seek more of it EVERY day!

My family experienced a house fire on April 30th, 1998, wherein we lost everything we owned. That forced my husband and I and all 9 kids, to live in two hotel rooms. This while seeking and, of course, not finding a house rental large enough, which fell within the budget. All eleven of us were living that way for two weeks before the next disaster struck.

Two weeks of replacing toothbrushes, underwear, jammies, combs, brushes, makeup, shampoo, and hair things. Each person needed a couple of changes of clothes. There were myriads of little details, including getting seven kids to and from six different schools daily, and the seemingly monumental task of feeding this large family, in a hotel. **PERSEVERANCE**.

It clearly had been a challenging two weeks and when I got back from work one evening, I could tell something else was wrong. It was quiet. No TV was on. No one was listening to music, loud or not. No one was talking. No one was arguing. Chilling…

I looked at my kid's father, nothing. I looked at each of my kid's sad, worried faces. Finally, 17-year-old David said, "Mom, your mom died." **CALM**.

I had not called to tell her of the house fire disaster. I had not called her in Texas to tell her how I was struggling to work, while looking for a house to rent, furniture to replace, beds for 11 people, their clothes, and other essentials. How my two youngest sons cried for the loss of Buzz Lightyear, Woody, and their other toys. How insult after insult on my soul were a constant barrage, I was barely getting through. It was not something I wanted to do, complaining to my parents. **FOCUS**.

I hadn't called her on Mother's Day the previous Sunday as I didn't have the energy to act like nothing was wrong and wish her a Happy Mother's Day. And now she was gone. My mom, my house, all our stuff, my plants, aquarium and fish, my kids' toys and now my soul, all felt gone.

It did not matter, what I was going through. It was on me to keep going. Do what needed to be done. Keep going for my kids. Let them see a responsible adult handling things for everyone. There wasn't time to grieve my loss of everything I had ever published, all my writing, my hand-me-downs from my mom and my mother, herself. There was not time for that. Grief had to wait. I had to make hard decisions and deal with them silently. I had to give myself grace to get through all of everything I was going through at once. **GRACE**.

In addition, to not going to my own mother's funeral in Texas, I had to deal with the anger from my father and my siblings for not being there. In case that sounds like I was heartless, let me share a few other details of this time.

Whoever called to tell me Mom had died, also put on my shoulders to tell my brother, Adam, who lived about 12 miles away from me. Not wanting to do that over the phone, I decided to drive out to his place that night, to tell him in person. My 15-year-old son, Stephan opted to go with me.

Adam was an over 6-foot tall, muscular dude who served in the US Army as a scout. He had always been a big, fit guy and was married to a local gal and had six kids. They lived on a plateau near the Green River outside of town. He and his then wife had worked hard to renovate their two-story house, creating a great place for a passel of kids to run wild being kids. They had animals and a 360-degree view of eastern Utah and western Colorado. The thought passed through my mind, driving out there, Adam would hold me, and we would grieve a little together, as we were far from the rest of the family and in the same boat being responsible for our large families.

Showing up at night with one kid was not a normal thing for me to do, so he knew something was up as soon as I walked in.

"Is it Dad?" he asked.

"Mom died," I responded, and walked in to hug him. Yet that didn't happen as I pictured it in my truck driving over. Adam collapsed to the floor with his hands on his face and keened. Crying out the word, "nooooo," he sobbed and sobbed on his knees. I didn't know what to do because I immediately felt responsible for his sorrow and was internally urged to forget my sorrow to help him.

In that moment, I recognized my whole family of father and siblings would expect me to step into Mom's shoes to handle details and their sorrows, and I decided not to. I had enough going on with our crisis of homelessness to take off for Texas. I was not going to subjugate myself to the needs of even more people while worrying about my kids, borrowing money for the trip, and losing the little income I made, which my family depended on solely, since John wasn't working then.

Have you noticed when you aren't a certain way, you don't think like other people, which can cause you to be blind-sided by their behavior? You can see, my default setting was to care for others, putting my needs aside consistently. Being excessively and unreasonably responsible, I reacted in ways no one else would.

Two of my brothers offered to pick me up in a motorhome they rented to drive to Texas from Salt Lake City. They drove through Vernal, where we were living, sort of, to pick up Adam and I for Mom's funeral. I was expected to pitch in on gas and rental, etcetera, with money I did not have, and I had already decided not to leave my kids in an even more unsettling situation. My brothers did not understand why I would not go, as if they ignored the situation I was already in with my immediate family. I listened to their criticism without defending myself and they left.

Then I got phone calls from my father and other brothers, reaming me for not coming to Mom's funeral. I had not anticipated their venom. Same thing. They ignored the crisis we were already in, trying to make me feel bad about myself on top of everything else. It was horrible. I would never have treated anyone like that.

No one reached out with concern for me and my family in our time of need. It was only criticism or zero contact. My family of origin ostracized me for years. There is more to this story, perhaps I will share another time. We have no control over how others choose to behave. We do have control over whether we accept their behavior or not, and I had not learned that lesson yet. I just kept going. **PERSEVERANCE**.

To get through tough times in our lives, we need to have the ability to cope in the moment. It's okay. I heard you swear under your breath there. I get it. Hard things happen and we keep going. We may not even think about our actions during a crisis, which are affecting others, let alone our long-term character growth! Yet, they may be the most important part of our battles. **PERSISTANCE**.

When we do life right, we learn from each experience, grow stronger, as better versions of ourselves. **TEACHABLE**.

All the things we do not tend to consider, while slogging through the morass of dumpster fire on top of dumpster fire, happening in our lives, matter. And that is the hope. Our struggles and how we navigate them, can inspire others. So, I suck up my pride and share with you. With the strength we develop of character traits, confidence, and faith, we can triumph over harsh situations which helps us to then thrive in our lives. **HOPEFUL**.

Cope, learn, grow, share, thrive became my life goals. Geez.

The traits we need, to go through this process are vast and many, yet can be simplified into specific character and personality traits, which can be developed. I did not realize there were so many when

I started writing this book with purpose. I also, am not good at editing the list down to a few, when they all seem so important.

Here are a few I started with, which answer, 'I am…' or 'I have…':

Adaptable	Grace	Perseverance
Adulting	Gratitude	Persistent
Boundaried	Happy	Perspective
Calm	Honest	Playful
Compassionate	Honor	Resourceful
Dependable	Hopeful	Responsible
Cooperative	Humble	Spiritual
Courage	Humor	Supportive
Creative	Inspire	Teachable
Curious	Intuitive	Thrifty
Diplomatic	Just	Tolerant
Efficient	Loyal	Trustworthy
Empathy	Observant	Unselfish
Flexible	Optimistic	Wise
Focus	Organized	
Generous	Patience	

Oh, for heaven's sakes what a long list! That's the tip of the iceberg!

There are many character and personality traits which can help you navigate life's challenges. Finding the right collection for you, in your life, is a great quest for you to launch. I highly recommend it. (You may start counting how many times I highly recommend something in the book, now! It means I know for a fact it works for me and may absolutely work for you, too!) **CURIOUS**.

CHAPTER 2

TO KNOW SOMETHING
OTHERS DON'T

*What can build resilience in our children and
grandchildren, are meaningful and strong relationships with other adults caring deeply about
them, and their lives, ergo grandparents, aunts,
uncles, cousins and other family and friends.*

What can build resilience in our children and grandchildren, are meaningful and strong relationships with
other adults caring deeply about them, and their lives,
ergo grandparents, aunts, uncles, cousins and other family and
friends.

I was sharing one of the funniest things that ever happened with
my kids with my daughter-in-law earlier today and realized the
difference perspective can make in a situation. It is a pure ego re-

action when something hard is happening to curl up in the fetal position, even if it is simply internally or emotionally, when it might be even more wise to take the opposite posture to puff up and stand for your rights. But being able to look at things from outside your fetal position can be extremely helpful because you just might not see what's really going on.

Case in point... Right after my divorce I was up early in the morning for work, coming home to get my kids from school, feeding them an early dinner, then heading off to college classes. So, I normally would get home sometime before 9:00 p.m. during the week. One hot summer evening, I called home before I left school to check on my kids, and my two youngest, Connor (five) and Danica (three) were starving to death, again, because it had been a couple of hours since they had eaten dinner.

I stopped by a pizza place to grab a pizza, then I swung by the house to grab the two of them, and we went to a park to sit and eat in the grass. The night was gorgeous as the sun was setting. It was during fire season in Utah, so the sunset was spectacular. I commented to my two youngest, "Oh my gosh you guys look at the sunset! The sky is gorgeous all fuchsia and tangerine!"

Connor glanced west, then made the comment, "much better than when you were a kid Mom, and the world was black and white." WISE.

What? Oh, my word that was so surprising to hear!

"Oh honey, the world wasn't black and white when I was a kid! We just hadn't figured out how to make film in color to capture it yet."

To which a surprised Connor gasped then exclaimed, "Oh! I know something other kids don't!"

That was some time ago because he just turned 29 last week and I still laugh out loud thinking of that story! From the mouths of babes...

Trauma can give us … Perspective.

There are myriads of ways to look at things. I cannot even begin to tell you all the crazy places my mind has gone over the years while dealing with crises. Anymore, the irony of things pretty much makes me laugh or my ironic comments make other people laugh in the moment. People might think I am irreverent or that I don't care, and they would be terribly wrong. I care too much which is why I use humor so often!

When a new parent is super excited about their brand-new baby boy this twisted thing inside of me generally wants to make some comment along the lines of, "Life as you know it is now over." "Get ready for all kinds of shenanigans you couldn't think of if you tried." "When Jason was in his coma... "

Truly, during an experience when my oldest son, Jason, was in a coma, after flying off his bullet bike, face first into a Lincoln in an intersection, when a lady illegally turned right in front of him, I had all kinds of experiences during those days afterwards. (Yes, I know I am the queen of run-on sentences. Breathe. You will be fine!)

Motorcycle accidents are no joke. The second day I was in the hospital with my son, his ICU nurse explained to me they call motorcycle accident victims with head trauma ODs. It stands for organ donor. Professionals assume if your motorcycle accident involves head injury, odds are good you're done. That wasn't the only experience I had during those days that was shocking and took my breath away. Yet, I'll share one story about perspective in hopes it will help you.

So, I had already been told by the resident doctor that, after their best efforts, Jason's prognosis was still death. That's nice to hear as a mom. I responded with, "You don't know this man. So, I will tell you if he wants to go, he will go. If he wants to stay, he will stay. And if he stays, he will hold you accountable for how you took care of him when he comes to."

I'm sure you can imagine he was hooked up to all manner of contraptions. Things on his calves which compressed to keep from stroke causing blood clots. Tubes down his throat. Tubes down his nose. A bolt literally screwed into the top of his skull. IVs with machines dinging and chirping and keeping track of everything, and technicians coming in and out to check on his status.

One morning, I walked in to find a handful of hospital clad people in his room, including a very tall resident doctor. Said doctor was bending over the machine monitoring Jason's breathing because although his heart was beating fine on its own, his lungs were struggling. Periodically, a very loud pop would echo inside the room which was a little disconcerting. I had no idea what it was, however, with the chatter amongst the staff, I picked up on the fact that my son was trying to breathe on top of the breathing machine. While still in a coma FYI.

Everybody was facing away from me looking at the machine when another loud pop happened. The resident doctor said, "I don't understand why he can't breathe in rhythm with the machine," to which I commented, "He can't dance either." **HUMOR**.

Well, it just fell out of my face. I still think it was damn funny! There was no thought to that whatsoever. In the moment, I was highly encouraged he was trying to breathe on his own while the professionals were frustrated, he wouldn't do it in rhythm with their machine. For heaven's sakes, people! WISE.

I chose the perspective of supreme gratitude in the improvement I was seeing, and he didn't have to match up to my textbook charts! GRATITUDE.

The intent of this book is to provide coping tools which work! Well, they have worked for me. Some of my tools have helped me develop the strong character traits I depend on no matter what comes up in my life. I am happy to share what has worked for me, as my hope is, they will work for you too, creating bridges to get from where you are to where you would like to be.

CHAPTER 3

WHEN NOTHING IS GOING RIGHT

*We all have moments when we fail to live up
to our principles. Humility is how quickly you
recognize it, and integrity is how hard you work to
rectify it.*

We all have moments when we fail to live up to our principles. Humility is how quickly you recognize it, and integrity is how hard you work to rectify it. To offer hope in hard and dark times is my intent here. I will keep reminding you this book is for you. It contains tough and very real stories along with workable solutions, yet, overall, the goal is for you to learn if others got through their -ish you can, too. Get ready for a roller coaster of emotional connection!

No matter what you are going through, with few exceptions, there is one piece of advice I recommend.

Choose gratitude.

Oh, believe me, I know that is not what you expected and perhaps not what you want to hear.

"Grateful. lady? Really? If I had something for which to be grateful, I would not be so miserable."

Is that how you feel all the time? Sometimes? Occasionally?

There is always something for which to be grateful. Always.

Years ago, when I was going through a dark time, enduring constant pain in my right knee, over such an extended period, changed my outlook on life. I was suffering with what my employment counselor called the 'worst case of corporate burn-out I've ever seen." I had just broken off a long-term relationship, sold my ish, packed the rest, grabbed my youngest, Danica, and moved across the country. I had no job and was burning through my bit of savings while applying for hundreds of possible work positions. **PERSISTENT**.

In Santa Cruz, California at the time, even part time jobs, with no benefits, were requiring master's degrees. I am talking about even an $11/hour receptionist position. And 200-600 people were applying for each one of those jobs.

Burned-out.

However, I had found something which worked for me in my attempt to cope with my life and that was Al-Anon, a 12-Step program for friends and families of alcoholics and addicts. I still use those tools daily without thinking about it. At that point in my life, I was down emotionally, mentally, spiritually. I was not sure even Al-Anon would be able to lift me up.

I got a new sponsor in Santa Cruz, whose first solution to turning my life around, was surprising to me. My Al-Anon sponsor recommended I start a gratitude list.

I had not heard of this before. She said I needed to write down thirty things, that very day, I was grateful for, and it could not, at that point, include people. No friends, no kids, no grandkids. I struggled. I was so stuck in the dense negativity of my life I could not think of anything to be grateful for. When I look back now, I find that kind of ridiculous, but stop the judging and remember what it was like. Depressing. I did it anyway. **RESPONSIBLE**.

I got a pad of paper and made a list of numbers 1 through 30 down the page.

I stared at the paper.

I stared off into the distance to the window.

I looked around my home and I noticed a paper clip on my desk.

Things I am grateful for:

- Number one - paper clips
- Safety pins
- Zippers
- Buttons

(I saw I was writing down things which hold stuff together and the irony was not lost on me! At a time when I could not hold my life together!) **HUMOR**.

- My pillow
- My bed
- The fact that I could go to a farmers' market and for four dollars get a big bunch of ranunculi to bring color into my home.

- Once a week I could go to the Hawaiian store and buy one lily, or one tuber rose which would make my entire home smell like heaven.

- My two tall wood backed olive green suede stools at my counter, which I found through Craigs List. I had to drive through the Santa Cruz mountains to pick them up and my friend Dave helped me. I still have them, and they and their memories make me smile.

- Friends of all kinds.

- That was not cheating because it was just a group not one individual.

- Standing on East Cliff and feeling the negative ions from waves of the Monterey Bay lapping on the shore.

- Doors with locks.

- My Toyota Tundra which has doors with locks. And windows and a corrugated bedliner so I can haul things without damaging them and how much I love driving my truck and how handy it has been for me in my life. It had suicide doors... so cool...

- My willingness to make substantial changes in life including moving across the country from Ogden, Utah to Santa Cruz, California.

- Being able to hear the surf while lying in my bed.

- My kids are resourceful and enterprising, creating their own independent lives.

- My pretty mango-colored dishes.

- My pretty hand-painted wine glasses.

- The daily farmers market in Capitola, which is open year-round, having low prices on all kinds of produce, seeds, nuts, and things I love to eat. (I am back to farmers markets!)

- Being able to eat healthy foods, easily and affordably, where I live.

- My ash gray Toms.

- The parts of my body which are healthy, pain-free, and strong.
- Very cool people I keep meeting in my life. I can learn from their experiences, things I would not normally see.

Making the commitment to myself to follow my wise Al-Anon sponsor's advice to take a month to do a gratitude list was working. It was not as hard to come up with things to add to the list now. I was starting each day thinking about what was good in my life and I finished each day doing the same. It was helping me. **FOCUS**.

Also, I was not judging myself for being ungrateful when I had so much going for me. I lived in a beautiful place where other people vacation. I was making friends who shared their experiences with me and places I had not seen yet, which I loved. I was developing healthier habits of attitude and eating and going through my life. **GRATITUDE**.

It got easier to get up in the morning. I began going to ten 12-step meetings a week. Al-Anon and some AA meetings, as many of my Santa Cruz friends seemed to be sober alcoholics. My social life became AA meetings, then lunch or meetings then dinner. In one such adventure, I was introduced to Green Chilis Soup and Avocado Soup. I was in heaven.

What am I grateful for this morning? I added:

- Avocado soup
- Breeze in my hair
- Hoodies to keep me warm when I'm letting the breeze blow in my hair.
- I recognize I don't speed when driving anymore. I believe it's because I'm where I want to be.
- Paddle boarding in the harbor alone or with a friend or family member.
- Locally owned restaurants.
- Locally owned coffee shops.

- Having skills, I can use to bless others' lives. **COMPASSIONATE.**
- Giving gifts for no reason.
- Realizing I don't need to swear as I have an extensive vocabulary and I'm smart enough to use it correctly.
- Cotton on my skin
- Linen on my skin
- Having a vehicle with a tailgate I can back onto the beach and drop to sit on and watch the surf. And the birds. And people. And smoke a clove. And drink alkaline water in my water bottle with a Peace symbol on it and be totally in the moment in nature.
- Having gifts from people reminding me I am loved when they are not around.
- Time spent with grandchildren.
- Being with my children and or their partners
- Facing the sun and feeling its warmth on my face
- Wiggling my toes into warm sand until they reach the cold damp sand underneath. **PLAYFUL.**
- Being near running water like rivers and streams
- Listening to the breeze in the tree leaves
- Learning something new
- Blending paint colors
- Seeing another human who smiles when seeing me
- Expressing myself in words
- Listening to music

Every day my sponsor admonished me to add another five things to my list and, over time, I went from small inanimate objects which made my life easier briefly, to deep emotional connection with others and the world around me. **SPIRITUAL.**

CHAPTER 4

AND THE BEAT GOES ON...

Train up a child in the way he should go and when
he is old, he will not depart from it.

PROVERBS 22:6 KJV

I did it for 30 days. For 30 days I added at least five new items to my gratitude list. At that point, my list was over 180 things for which I was grateful, because I didn't stop with the recommended numbers. And then, that month. I realized how very blessed I was and how much I had to be grateful for and how many things were not even on my list yet. **GRATITUDE**.

Previously, I had been focused on constant pain in my knee, zero to small income, did not feel stable in my life, and was a two days drive away from my family and Utah friends, feeling lonely and small. I was empty nesting a couple years too soon and could not seem to snap out of it, on top of debilitating corporate burn out. I was going through the motions with a career counselor through the state, who was patient and consistent which was exactly what I needed.

The most interesting little opportunities came my way, like a sweet friend asking me if I would housesit while she was away on a work trip. So, I got to stay in her lovely home, take care of her pet, and enjoy her Koi Pond and private backyard. **HOPEFUL**.

That opened another opportunity to housesit for four months in another lovely home. There were challenges. There was family drama with the homeowner making it easy for me to slip into negativity and feel picked on for little reason. Instead, I had to develop coping skills, to navigate and move through it with some clumsy attempt at grace. **HUMBLE**.

This is how I learned, though. Nothing was perfect, yet there were blessings everywhere. A dear friend/adopted brother, Kim, asked me to help with his bookkeeping, giving me enough money to put gas in my truck. This meant I could go to the local farmers market, for food and fun. We struck a deal wherein he gave me grocery money, I shopped and prepared meals for us throughout the week. He did not eat alone, and I got to do something I love and share it. It was a big blessing. **RESPONSIBLE**.

I saw an improvement over my previous married life, where it was always a battle to get grocery money and I had to justify why I needed pads or tampons. I did not have to fight for diapers or diaper wipes, yet anything purchased for me personally, was a challenge. With meals with Kim, it was the opposite. Fair and equitable. He financed our daily meals; I shopped and prepared them for us. Perfectly fair! And I was grateful.

• Meals with Kim

One of my coping mechanisms, not to be confused with denial (insert cheesy grin here), was to think of parts of my life, in the third person. Like this:

Her kids' father was not allowed to call her. That was not set up immediately after the divorce, but sometime later when verbal abuse became so much, she created a boundary for him. The only reason he was allowed to call her was if something serious was going on with one of their kids.

It was 8:30 at night, and her bag was packed for a trip into the city for the next day, for a business presentation. She had made arrangements for each of her kids to spend the night at one of their friends, in town, and her plan was to be back the day after next.

But she was waiting for her 16-year-old son to get back with her truck and get everybody tucked in for the night. He was late. It always made her nervous when any of her kids were not home on time. And then her phone rang. Thinking it was Alex with an excuse for why he wasn't there, yet, she grabbed it and answered, "hello."

"Jason's been in a motorcycle accident, and you need to get down here to say goodbye to him," was the first thing out of her kids' father's mouth.

Reality hit and I snapped into the present.

"What happened? "I asked.

"I just told you. He's been in a bad accident, and you need to get down here so they can pull the plug."

In the next hour, I packed a bigger bag with more clothes, considered taking my truck and driving 14 hours straight to Tucson, through the night. I called the various people who were going to be watching my kids for one overnight to see if my kids could stay longer, letting them know what had happened.

Called the hospital where my son, Jason, was to see if I could get any more information.

Called his brothers who were in Tucson to see what I could find out.

Alex came home with my truck. I told him what was going on and he wanted to come to Tucson with me. I told him, "I need you here to oversee everything with the kids, Alex. I don't know what I'm walking into down there and they're not gonna let you into Intensive Care Unit at 16-years-old. I'm sorry. I do need you here."

I got the kids down to bed and then it was getting pretty late, yet I called my friend Kori, anyway.

When she and I hung out around town sometimes, people would come up to me because I was very well known, but if people came up to Kori, it was a very different experience. Kori worked as a CNA; certified nursing assistant I think it stands for. She worked in hospice, helping people navigate the last days of their lives and helping their families. When we ran into people who knew her from her job, I got the strong sense they thought she was an angel on earth. So, of course, I called her.

"Apparently Jason's been in a bad motorcycle accident, and I have not been able to find the details from anyone coherent. I have got to go to Tucson, so I'm packing my truck."

"You are not driving to Tucson tonight in this state. You need to get some rest and make the trip tomorrow by plane."

"I don't have the money for that," I said. "It sounds really serious, and I better get there as soon as I can and I don't know how long I'll have to be there either, so I'd like to have my truck," I responded.

"You focus on trying to get some sleep tonight, which I know is going to be tough, and don't worry about it. I'm going to make some calls," she said.

The next day, an employee of one of the local companies picked me up to drive me to the Salt Lake airport, with a one-way ticket to Tucson. It was paid for by the owner of that company.

The kid didn't know why he was taking me to the airport, so he was a chatty Cathy for the whole 3 1/2-hour trip! It helped take my mind off of things here and there and he didn't mind me being quiet.

I went through the motions at the airport until I got seated on the airplane next to a Delta employee, who was just taking a trip herself. Once the plane started taking off, I leaned my head back into my seat and could not hold the tears back anymore. They just flew down my face in silence.

The Delta employee was not clueless, and I don't even remember what she said to me, but I told her my son had been in an accident and I didn't know what I was walking into. The stranger took my hand and prayed for me sitting right there on the plane. I wiped my eyes. I wiped my nose. I wiped my nose again. And then I wiped my eyes again and she gave me my hand back as the process was a two-handed job, at this point. And I will never forget her kindness and gentleness in such a hard time.

In the meantime, my sons had arranged for me to stay with friends of Jason's and one of them picked me up at the airport. Even in my barely contained, distracted state, I could tell the dude was on some kind of drugs. So, I kept my luggage with me when he dropped me off at the hospital.

My son was in the Intensive Care Unit, on the fifth floor of the University of Arizona Medical Center. I got off the elevator with my luggage and started down the long corridor. I could see something dark in the floor of a doorway up ahead and as I got closer, I saw it was a pant leg.

It was my second oldest son, Trevor, dressed for work, sitting in the doorway crying. He got up when he saw it was me and hugged me and sobbed. Trevor, at 22 years-old, was a pretty tough cookie, so to see him so distraught made me think this might be as bad as his father said.

Trevor walked me to the locked doors, where we had to speak through an intercom to be let in. When we got to Jason's room, I set my luggage against the wall and didn't even recognize my son in the hospital bed. He was about 30 pounds heavier than normal and connected to all manner of machines. Dried blood was caked to his face, head, and various body parts. Then I looked around the room at his three brothers and his father and looked back at Jason in the hospital bed.

An objective observer would have instantly known this wasn't good. There were things attached to all parts of his body. There were things squeezing his calves to keep blood clots from forming. He had IVs in his arms to give him fluids and other things. He had a bolt screwed into his skull attached to a machine. He had things in his nose, and things in his mouth, and clamped down on his fingers, and a catheter attached to a bag. All of these things were connected to machinery and other things in the room and at this moment there was no staff in there.

Everyone was silent. And I instantly knew Jason was not gone. I sensed his spirit, and I knew he was there with his body. That wasn't something that I normally experienced, but I knew it was true. So, I said so. His father said, "he lost his eyesight and is going to be permanently blind in at least one eye."

It didn't take him much longer to say there was no point to hanging around the hospital room and he left. I found out later he actually got on a plane and went back to San Francisco where he was working so he wasn't kidding about not hanging out at the hospital! That actually uncomplicated things a bit.

CHAPTER 5

UNSHELTERED & GIFTS

*Character is striving to become the person you
claim to be.*

—ADAM GRANT

The boys and I stood around Jason's bed after their father left, contemplating Jason losing his eyesight in at least one eye. We looked at each other, thinking and wondering, and then the conversation started.

"He'll probably get a cat eye," said one brother.

"Nah, He hates cats."

"He'll probably get a lizard eye like an iguana or something."

We all paused to consider Jason's glass eyeball options and then I said, "he'll probably get a multi-sided die which will flip around with different numbers on, it to entertain people, when he's playing dungeons and dragons."

I think the hospital staff listening to this, were horrified, not understanding humor is definitely a default for Cross family crises. **HUMOR**.

I learned that the Intensive Care Unit nurses worked three 12-hour shifts for three days in a row. The first nurse I met was a retired firefighter who went back to school to be a nurse and was a pretty cool dude. He had a little bit of compassion, and he also didn't pull punches. He answered my questions including what in the hell was the bolt screwed into Jason's head for.

He showed me the machine the bolt was connected to which had two graphs on a screen. One was for the right hemisphere of his brain and the other was for the left hemisphere of his brain. I could immediately see there was minimal activity on the right side and less than minimal activity on the left side. The nurse wanted me to understand their expectation for Jason coming out of this accident, was about zero. **COURAGE**.

I have to share what my friend Kori told me on the phone the night of Jason's accident, because it came back to me in the hospital room. She told me a couple of things.

First of all, head injury victims do not like to be touched physically. It's highly irritating to their nervous systems. So, she said, "I know you won't be able to not touch him, so find a place on his forearm where you can just put your hand firmly, but not hard, and just hold still."

Dad had taught me about a healing touch when I was a teenager. You don't touch roughly, and you don't touch too lightly, because both of those are irritating. You touch with a firm healing touch. It was hard to find a spot on Jason's forearm that wasn't attached to something, but I found a spot, and when I touched him with a firm healing touch, I watched the graphs to see if it would affect him negatively or positively.

At first, it didn't seem to have any effect, so I thought it was a safe thing to do. But when I noticed, after a few hours, more activity on both sides of his brain, there was nothing that was going to keep me from not touching my son!

Kori also taught me, when someone is leaving this planet, the last sense to stop working is hearing, and it becomes very acute, and they can hear things way down the hallway, let alone anything going on in their room. So, she said, "make sure everything that is said in that room is positive and even out in the hallway, because he can hear that."

My dear friend, Kori, also gave me another really hard piece of advice to hear. She said, "when you get the chance you tell Jason, 'If you want to go, you go. We will be OK. If you want to stay, you stay. And we will all be OK. The choice is yours. This is your life.'"

Before Jason's nurse kicked me out of his room for the night, he told me a couple of things. First of all, he said motorcycle head injury victims have a nickname in hospitals. They are called OD's. It stands for 'organ donors.' That was a wakeup call, let me tell you.

The other thing he told me was that every night I had to go home or wherever I was staying. I had to eat dinner. I had to take a shower or a bath. Go swimming if I could. And I could come back the next morning, and I could stay all day, but every night I had to go home and get some sleep. He said, "if he does come to, he's going to need you, and you need to have your energy." 'If', he said. I thought, 'when' he comes to.

I had told my boys I didn't want to stay with Jason's friends and why. I did not live a life around drugs, and wasn't about to start it now. I asked if I could stay with Jason's girlfriend, Ronnal and her son, a cute little four-year-old redheaded boy! The boys made the arrangements, and she came and picked me up at 6:30pm, when the nurse chased me out. I took my luggage and was grateful for her generosity.

The entire time I was in Tucson this trip, I stayed with Ronnal. I had no idea just how generous she was being to me because she never told me she and Jason had broken up months before. Nobody bothered to tell me! She just opened her home to me, fed me, let me take her car when I dropped her off at work, so I could go to the hospital every day and then I would pick her up after she got off work. **GRATITUDE**.

SUMMER 2012

All my experiences of Jason's motorcycle accident were long before I learned about a Gratitude List or Journal and yet I believe it is human nature to search for the silver lining or light at the end of the tunnel or some such metaphor when life feels impossible. It felt similar to the time in Santa Cruz when I was running out of options, with no resources to fix things.

Living in Santa Cruz, California, I was one week out from the house-sitting opportunity I had for four months, while the owners were on their boat in the Caribbean. The homeowners were coming home, and I still did not have a job, nor did I have a place to live, nor money to pay for a place to live, when a stranger gave me a call.

She was a friend of my Koi Pond friend, Giovanna, and said, "I understand you need a place to live. I bought a home and rent it to my ex-husband and in the back there's a guest house which I cannot legally rent because no permits were purchased before it was originally built. Would you like to see it?"

I paid her $400 a month cash and it included my utilities for a lovely self-contained bungalow in a safe neighborhood. The container gardens I built that summer thrived on my little 10-foot deck and I grew my own tomatoes, peppers, strawberries, and herbs. You can see videos of this bountiful time on my YouTube channel, roxy-crossdesigns. It has over 40 videos on how to grow food and flower plants together in gorgeous baskets and planters, from the Bloom Master company, yet I digress… **HAPPY**.

Who lives in the expensive area of Santa Cruz, California for $400 a month? It was a blessing! And those few months were good times. I was five minutes from the beach, I was close to downtown, and I was able to afford the things I needed. **GRATITUDE**.

I volunteered at the MAH. The Santa Cruz Museum of Art and History. Volunteers got in for free. Once or twice a month there were events I got to help with. They loved me because I had a truck and could haul treasures here and there. I could not stand for long because of my injured knee, but I could drive my truck to help. **COOPERATIVE**.

Volunteering at the museum was fun. Before then, I had always volunteered in community, serving as a trustee on boards of the county or nonprofits. These boards worked for noble causes, but it became emotionally difficult. The county library was okay. I created and ran a kids creative writing contest for well over a year, maybe two, while serving. That was fun! Then my service got more intense.

1998

I worked for over six years as a trustee on the Uintah County Public Lands Committee. This was demanding, working long hours creating county public land policy for the county, often at odds with federal government agencies. It was a fascinating and critically important effort. I even ran for Uintah County Commission to protect the county land rights at one point. **COOPERATIVE**.

SPRING 2003

Later, when I moved to Salt Lake City, I served on another non-profit board, protecting the rights of injured people in the State of Utah. Our board meetings were full of people in wheelchairs and others, telling their heart wrenching stories. **COMPASSIONATE**.

APRIL 2011

With other experiences like that, I felt when I got to Santa Cruz, it was time to do something fun, so I did. I was learning. It was okay to volunteer my time for something fun. Fun is important, too! And God knows I needed less unnecessary work and stress and more fun in my life! I was creating boundaries with my time and efforts. **ADAPTABLE**.

It is amazing how little energy a person can have when they are exhausted from not having boundaries and sticking to them. I did not say, "no" to pretty much anything for years, and took on way more responsibility than I had time and energy for, which I could see at that point. Through counseling and a wise Al-Anon sponsor, I was using the tools I was learning.

OCTOBER 2010

I discovered Al-Anon because of a dear friend and had never heard of it before. My daughter, Danica and I were vacationing in Park City, Utah while I contemplated leaving a long-term relationship. I found it was a 12-step program for friends and family members of alcoholics and addicts. I did not know at the time I had been surrounded by alcoholics and addicts my whole life. I did not understand how it worked. I did have the sense I should follow up with this program and learn what I could. **INTUITIVE**.

I went to meetings and had multiple sponsors over the years working on different things in my life. That program has given me tools

I still use every single day without even thinking anymore because they apply to so many circumstances and issues.

I learned to adapt them to my life. When I was driving and everyone around me was being slow, in my own mind, I would use a version of the serenity prayer saying, "God, bless me with the patience to deal with these drivers!" And a serious sanity saver was learning to say, "no." "No." "No!"

Try it.

Right now.

Say, "no!" Do it again! Now say, "No!" to the next five things you get asked to do. I dare you! Tell me how that goes! I believe in you! **INSPIRE**.

I learned it is not my responsibility to fix everything that's broken in the world. And I don't have to say, "yes" to everything people ask me to do, to be a good person in God's eyes. **CONSISTENT**.

It was during this time I also started a bucket list. Previously I had never been able to envision myself into the future. I felt if I started writing down things I wanted to see or do or experience during my life I might be able to draw those things to me. There were things I wanted to learn. There were places I wanted to visit. And there were many experiences I wanted to have. In making that list it did not even occur to me I might be able to start marking things off my list right away! I was taking it 'One Day at a Time' yet starting to see light around the edges of my life. **HOPEFUL**.

CHAPTER 6

FROM DREAD TO BUCKET LIST

*The fear of failure for me was overshadowed by the
excitement of doing what I love, there is always
that little bit of fear in the background, but it can
be balanced with your reason for doing it.*
—STEPHEN FOURIE

A friend asked if I wanted to take a day to drive up the coast, and before I knew it, I was crossing over the Golden Gate bridge visiting harbors and beautiful little towns on the other side and coming back over the other bridge to experience a lovely day in conversation and learning new things. **CURIOUS**.

Another dear friend, whom I think of as my adopted older brother, Kim, took me to San Francisco one Sunday to experience a gospel church choir. Glide Memorial. It is famous so you can look it up if you like. I had always wanted to be in the room with a black gospel choir. Their passion and intensity when singing about the Lord was something I wanted to experience! It was fabulous, and I loved being in a congregation of diversity with gorgeous stained-glass windows and the old wooden pews of such a great old church. **GRACE.**

Then even though it was difficult for me to walk, we went to Fisherman's wharf and experienced a variety of street performers and colorful booths and had clam chowder! Clam chowder at Fisherman's wharf and listening to a fabulous Gospel choir were two things on my bucket list I could mark off in one day! Very grateful girl and absolutely present in the moment that day! **GRATITUDE.**

That happened to be the day my wise Al Anon sponsor had said I need to write 30 things I was grateful for before the end of the day and it was the beginning of another level of learning for me. By choosing Gratitude daily, morning and night life did get better. And when things get hard, I do this all over again. I have a Gratitude Journal now and my goal is to fill it before my next birthday. With all the blessings in my life, I should be able to do that in a year! Here is another tiny tool which helped keep my sanity.

Have you ever been in such a dark place breathing is actually difficult? You hold your breath, and you just keep holding? Perhaps you're in that spot now.

Here's a tip of what I did when I was in that circumstance. I tore off the corner of a little piece of paper and wrote one word on said paper. "Breathe." Then I stuck the paper in my pocket of whatever I was wearing that day because I knew during the course of the day I would stick my hand in my pocket, feel the paper, and be reminded. See, when you're under stress it is very easy to forget breathing has two parts. Under stress we are really good at taking a breath in and holding it. And holding it. And holding it. It is so important to be reminded to let it go.

Breathing has two parts. The second part of breathing is exhaling. Yeah, you needed that reminder didn't you! **PERSEVERANT.**

I told you, I like paperclips, those little wires holding things together. Pretty sure there's some sort of analogy to my life in there or lack of holding things together more likely!

What else is handy and holds things together? Safety pins. Reminds me of diapering my siblings back before disposable diapers were invented. I even used them for the first month after I had my oldest son Jason because some sweet soul gave me access to a diaper service for the first month of his life. So, cloth diapers safety pins, and rubber pants it was. Are you old enough to remember that ceremony repeated throughout every dang day when you had a baby? Ask your mom or your grandma about it!

SIDENOTE: stinky cloth diapers get rinsed out in toilets by hand which is a task I started doing for my mother with my siblings when I was seven. Consider your ancestors and what they used to have to do daily to survive… There are blessings to count in there, galore!

Looking around, I see the zipper on my hoodie and add zippers to the list. Buttons on my shirt cuff and I add buttons to the list. I had four things on my gratitude list at this point and only 26 more to go before I went to bed that night. Little things holding life together.

What is holding your life together? Want to hear more?

If you think I learned a cool tool and smoothly used it after that without stumbling, you are incorrect. I stumbled all over the place and publicly, too. Much of my adult life I have been anywhere on a spectrum from the public eye to small town celebrity. One morning, I got a call from a friend asking whose truck was parked in my driveway and who was the man scraping snow off my Tundra. That was from driving on a main street, glancing down the road I lived on. And darned if she wasn't right! Some guy was egging for brownie points in front of my house! Even that little incident embarrassed me. I was a single woman with little kids, working in media, and did not want public gossip about who was parked in my driveway early in the morning. Geez. **HUMBLE**.

During all the comings and goings of crisis and such in my life, I have been deeply challenged by faith. Not to be confused with religion, which I did battle with, but faith. I came to a place dealing with Jason's coma where I could no long deny something bigger than me was at work. That man, my oldest son, should have been dead for at least seven reasons I could count, yet he wasn't. He not only was not dead, although he did change in personality and some habits, he is still smart, hardworking, and keeping the same job for some time now. My faith began to grow. I recognized miracles all around me. **SPIRITUAL**.

Now I have to tell you something kind of funny that was a clear indication of how my mind was not functioning correctly, when I heard about my son Jason's motorcycle accident. Back to that time…

I got to Ronnal's house, and she showed me where I would be sleeping. I put my suitcase on the bed then opened it up to pull out something clean to put on after a shower only there were zero pairs of panties in my luggage. None! Not one single pair!

There were five pairs of sandals and shoes in there, not including the ones I was wearing. There were mismatched outfits and tops and shorts and a couple of dresses and just the bra I was wearing. No pajamas. No big T-shirt to wear to sleep in. I don't know where the hell my brain was when I was packing the suitcase, but it wasn't matching outfits and making sure I had everything I needed!

So, I had to look at what else I had packed in the way of toiletries to see what was missing and what I needed to go buy! Five pairs of shoes and no underwear! Also, no swimsuit, which is always the first thing going in my suitcase when I travel! I made a list of things I needed to get that night, and Ronnal gave me her car keys to go to Target.

I bought toiletries, pairs of thongs, and a couple of summer shirts and a pair of shorts that would match the stuff I brought with me. That helped me relax that night and sleep.

The next morning when I woke up, I discovered my period had started in the night! Good Lord! Seriously?

I had to borrow some tampons and pads from Ronnal and run back to target to buy regular panties which would hold sticky pads, and for convenience I went into the infant section and bought a big container of diaper wipes. Then I got a box of Ziploc bags, chocolate, and a bag of crunchy Cheetos. That's what I thought I needed for this day.

Amazing how having to deal with something is mundane and inconvenient as a menstrual period can take your mind off of the trauma of having a son everyone else thinks is going to die, for heaven's sakes! **PERSEVERANT**.

CHAPTER 7

CATASTROPHY MAGNET

*Sometimes you get the best light from a burning
bridge.*

—DON HENLEY

It probably used to be easier to talk about faith. More people were faith-based. They went to church. They read their holy books. They prayed, and observed religious holidays, ceremonies, and observances. They said, "You are in our prayers" and no one made fun of them. I remember hearing a Black single mom talk about Jesus when I was a young woman and I marveled at how strongly she felt and the passion she had for her faith. I felt she knew Jesus and wondered why white people do not sound like her when they talk about their beliefs. **SPIRITUAL**.

Now don't get in a tizzy. We are always able to learn new information and perspectives when we are open to it. Why it seems more prevalent with youth I do not know. I love to learn. It is a key part of who I am. One of the questions I always asked when getting to know someone new, is "what do you like to read?" A response like, "oh I don't read books" will lose my interest instantly in a new suitor. That won't fit! I had read over 10,000 books by the time I was 50! Obsessive much? Who cares? It is my life and I love to learn. **TEACHABLE**.

Then there are the times I learn by experience, and I tap in hard to what I have learned from others, through books, programs, coaching and life in general. Life is challenging enough, let alone when you let others into your life. There is nothing like your own children and grandkids to give your heart and soul a run for their money.

Jason, my oldest hit a moving vehicle directly with his face. No one knows to this day why he was not wearing a helmet, which according to his doctor, saved him from breaking his neck and probably killing him.

He suffered anaphylactic shock from a plasma infusion in the emergency room! Who is allergic to plasma? Apparently, I am too, yet that is another story. Those are just a couple of the seven things I know of, which tried to kill him in his motorcycle incident. Years later, November 8th, 2018, to be exact, Jason lived through the fire which destroyed Paradise and Magalia, California, which was such an ordeal I have no descriptive words for you.

My friend, Steve, called from California to ask me if my son was okay. I have seven of them so I asked, "which one?" "The one who lives just north of me where everything is on fire." I was in the airport in Austin TX waiting to board, knowing I was going to be incommunicado for over four hours, so I hung up and called Jason. Nothing. I called his girlfriend. Nothing. I left a voicemail on both phones and then text them both. I know big fires take out cell towers. My inner conversations were how resilient Jason was and how savvy of a survivor he had always been.

I thought of what his options might be, assuming he had any, and chose to believe he would easily grab family, camping gear, water, and whatever tools he had time for and would head into the Sierra Nevada mountains and even over the mountains to Reno. I tried to convince myself Jason was fine and handling trauma with grace and aplomb. Well maybe with a lot of swearing actually, but handling things better than most people would.

That did not help the hours and hours I suffered with not knowing he was okay, with not being able to hear his voice. **PERSEVERANCE**.

The plane home boarded and as hard as it was, I put my phone on airplane mode, then tried to read and look at the window while tears randomly fell down my face on and off during the flight. It looked like I read the airline magazine cover to cover yet I could not tell you one thing in it by the time we landed.

The second we touched down I turned my phone on, willing it to provide me with a voicemail. A text. Nothing. I gathered belongings, picked up luggage which I schlepped to the bus to take me to my car. Nothing. Turned the phone volume as high as it would go, then drove home. I checked with my other kids; most had not heard about the fire. Now I had them concerned, although they reminded me, as Jason had after surgeries from the motorcycle accident, "You can't hurt titanium." Yah, well you can melt it, I thought.

This kind of life trauma is seriously tough to plough through. The mind weasels take over, spinning their 'what ifs' until I can't breathe. At home, alone, I knew I had to take some kind of smart action until I heard something. **HOPEFUL**.

Airline almonds were all I had eaten, and it was past dinner time at this point. I blended a protein shake for the creamy deliciousness, the nutrition, and because when you are sipping or drinking something you have to breathe. You have to slow down and pay attention, so you don't spill on yourself and clothes. I thought about that telling myself to be in the moment. I thought of the words of Byron Katie. Did I know for a fact Jason was in danger? Was he even in town at the time? Was he doing a custom furniture job in San Diego as he often did? Where they on vacation in Tucson where his girlfriend's mom lived? Vacation meant phones off. Did he see what was happening and go uphill into the Sierra Nevadas headed to Reno? Maybe he was on his way to Utah where his siblings and I were?

Jason is a smart camper. He can fish, and make things work, and is generally prepared for what can come his way. I pictured him gathering Shannon and her two kids and four rescue dogs and heading into the 'high ups'. I felt that is what he would do, avoiding fire and masses of people who don't know what to do. The story I told myself was that he was safe and invigorated by outsmarting Mother Nature or whatever or whomever had started the fire in the first place.

I kept using storytelling to calm myself when there was nothing I could do except wait. Thousands of people were in crisis, injured and dead in northern California that day. Emergency personnel were far beyond capacity. The wise action was to remain calm and wait.

Being able to remain calm in a crisis is a superpower. **CALM**.

CHAPTER 8

THE PHONE RINGS

God will only give you what you would have asked
for if you knew everything he knows.
—TIMOTHY KELLER

Even when God is in charge, people lose their freedom, they starve, they die, and hearts get broken. But that is not because of God. It is because of people's choices and people around them and their choices and consequences to said choices. God gives us strength to get through hard times yet does not necessarily remove them.

Two of my siblings called me last night. First, Val and then Jeff. We talked for a long time about a lot of important things, and I was grateful as it was an amazing experience with both of them.

Jeff talked about the trauma of our childhood and losing two of our younger brothers within a year last year and questioning things we will never know the answers to because our parents are gone. I told him I asked Dad hard questions before he died, and he did not answer me, so I tried. Dad stared off into space when I asked how I really got the burn scars on my body. The stories my mother told when I asked as a child make no sense as a grown adult. There are secrets in our family, and they died with our parents.

Now, it is expected of us, as the oldest, to carry on in certain ways when neither of us had the energy nor the interest. He said we have to live at least to 68 to break that dying from a young age we dealt with, with our mother.

Mom died when she was my age, which I am very aware of this year. It is spooky. I have tried to talk about it, yet people do not understand my concerns, so I do not bring it up anymore. One of my children said, "aging is a blessing denied to many" or something along those lines which was not what I was talking about. Better to keep things to myself than trigger others. **ADULTING**. (You probably won't find 'adulting' on a character trait list however it is a common term my youngest uses and it fits. Meaning doing what needs to be done regardless of what you want to do.)

It was surprising to find my brother is as concerned as I am about that 67 number. That is way too young to die, and I am still not okay, although Mom left the planet over 24 years ago. It does not go away, which is why Dr Brene' Brown talks about grace during the grieving process. There is no timeline for grief ending. Just feel it, let it move through you, and it should get better. Over time. I was really glad my brother called. **GRACE**.

I had a dream last night that I was trying to drive south on I-15 in the middle of nowhere with no cell service and I was stopped by US military forces. They would not let me continue south. They would not let me cross over the grassy median to go back north. And they did not want me to stay parked in front of them. No reasonable options in this dream. Probably more of a nightmare rated PG-13. One of the vehicles had a big machine gun on top. I looked the soldier who stopped me, right in the eyes, and told him to do the next right thing and then I woke up.

Do the next right thing. Where did I learn that phrase? It is a good one. When I was working so hard not to lose my mind waiting to hear from Jason during what the media called the Camp Fire, I was doing the next right thing. Nothing. I left the emergency people alone, kept my phone charged and prayed. Not a crazy, 'you have to fix this' prayer like my normal ones. I prayed a simple, "Bless Jason. Bless Shannon. Bless Kaylie and Chris and their dogs."

Calling that fire the 'Camp Fire' was so deceptive. There was a spot on the map called Camp, so they used that as the name, which to the rest of the world sounds like some camper did not extinguish their campfire. Not what happened at all. But I digress again.

And then my phone rang. Jason's cell.

"Hello…"

"Mom. It was raining fire. Raining Fire. *RAINING FIRE*. Pieces of melting plastic and rubber were falling on us. We had to watch where we put our feet and all around us and up above because IT WAS RAINING FIRE, MOM…"

He went on forever, in detail of what they experienced from sensing something was wrong in the morning, to filling cars with essentials only to not be able to go anywhere when they got to a major road.

People were just stopped.

Soon it was black as night in the morning. They grabbed backpack, purse, a preteen and barely teen and four rescue dogs and walked. No idea if they were walking into danger or away from it or if there was any safe direction. Fire was burning all around them and falling from the sky.

Jason looked for pennants. The kind they use to indicate chemicals used on your lawn, to see which way the wind was blowing. Chris, the youngest lagged behind until Jason yelled, "Is this the day you die, Chris? Stay with your mother!" Which he did for the rest of the ordeal. **ADULTING**.

Doing what has to be done, saying what has to be said, like it or not.

When you are unprepared for catastrophic events, you better have excellent character traits to keep you alive. And to not put others at risk. What parent is going to let a kid wander off because they refuse to mind? When life gets serious, you have to make the hard decisions and then live with them. If you live.

They got picked up hours later and were taken to a home in Chico and then they were evacuated from that area as emergency personnel were not sure if it was safe there from the still burning fires.

"It was raining fire, Mom. Disaster movies are ruined for me, forever." "For ev er…"

He is his mother's son. He was dead serious, and yet his method of communicating his ordeal had intelligent humor in it. **HUMOR**.

Disasters happen, and until it happens to you, or worse, a loved one, it is hard to comprehend. Hard things come our way and life keeps going. Life does not stop because we are traumatized. It plows along, and we can stay stuck in the morass or figure out how to move on with it. Whatever help we need, we should grab.

Counseling, or coaching with someone who can help you is great. So is having good friends and family support. My intent has been to be there for the people I love. That has meant I HAD to learn how to understand and control my fears. This is an on-going process which has been exhausting at times.

Remaining calm, pausing before acting or reacting, has been a solid trait I have developed, yet not perfected. I'm human. It involves being patient. Pausing for others to have time to figure out what they need to, without always butting in, is another trait I have worked on at length. There have been many times I was polite when I should have let someone have it, for their horrid behavior. Yet when the best path is not clear, I err on the side of pausing and remaining calm. I can always choose to act later. **CALM**.

Because the really hard life experiences I have endured, and/or endured on behalf of friends and family, have been brutal, I recognize that reality, no matter how often I tend to find humor in them. None of these stories would have humor if Jason and my other kids had not lived. With all the things my family has been through, it is a miracle we are still alive and even thriving in most cases. **GRATITUDE**.

CHAPTER 9

DATING AND MEN'S BAD BEHAVIOR

Don't mistake a lapse in judgment
for a lack of character.

There was a time in my life, where I wondered if there is something about me that causes people to show their true colors, which are sometimes kind of ugly. There was a whole period of time when I was the magnet for unhappily married men. Man, I thought that was disgusting, and had a really hard time being civil and feeling good about myself. I was raised to be civil, no matter what, and yet I have such strong beliefs on fidelity of marriage, I reacted inside. And their creepy behavior made me feel dirty, which was not deserved. **BOUNDARIED**.

That period of time would have been a good time to hear this quote from Helen Mirren, "Women have got to stop being polite. If I ever had children, which I don't, the first thing I'd teach a girl of mine is the words 'f - off." I believe there is another quote of hers about the one thing she has learned with aging is she should have said, 'f – off' more often. There has to be a way to adapt that to my life.

When we are approached by unacceptable behavior, it sure can make us feel like we are dirty, if we are not careful. Here I was a single woman, well known in the community, trying to work to support my children, with no assistance of any kind, and these jackasses were doing things I felt were going to tarnish my reputation. Disgusting. **HONOR**.

I had a couple of long-term relationships since my divorce but nothing in the last 12 years. I did not date for five years and then I tried it for a month and quit. The next year, I tried it again for three months, giving it my best shot and then quit. And when I tried it for the third year in a row, in October, I thought, "what is this weird pattern?"

Then I read an article, I can no longer locate, which said there is a phenomenon, in October, people start looking for a partner, so they do not go through the holidays alone. I had to meditate on that for a little bit to see if I was in that pattern. And I might have been.

This year, I did not join a dating site because I have found them supremely depressing. They seem to be a collection of very unhappy old men. When I last stuck my toe in the dating pool, in fall of 2020, I met one man after another with big issues I did not want to take on. I admit it. **RESPONSIBLE**.

The guy I went out with who stuck a pistol in the door pocket of my car so I would be safe, was one, for instance. Because both of his vehicles, and about every room in his house, had weapons, apparently, so he would feel safe. I guess this meant he thought everyone should do the same. That did not transfer to giving one to me! Especially not without a discussion. I do not have feelings against guns, it is simply a topic important enough to discuss not foist on me, and I did not want to be beholding to him for any reason.

Then there was the guy before that, who neglected to mention several serious health conditions, which is an issue to me because I'm very transparent, forthright, and honest about such things.

If I had been with the man for years, creating a life, and then health issues came up, that's one thing. To walk into them cold, at this point in my life, is another. To paint a picture of a specific kind of life, only for me to find out fairly quickly, it was far from accurate currently, is another huge red relationship flag. How about finding out someone has a contagious disease, they could share with you, which fortunately I did not catch! Or what about this idea, I am expected to be monogamous, yet he certainly is not. Right when I think I have seen it all, I see something else weird. **RESPONSIBLE**.

I have now been divorced longer than I was married to my children's father, and rarely think about the brief marriage I had after that, with someone who was deceptive and unsupportive. My idea of creating a blended family and putting my all into a relationship was not matched in any way, shape, or form.

Then to hear one of my brothers compare me to our Grandma Pearl, who never married or even dated after the death of her husband, at 45 years old, was a bit eye opening. That was surprising and not all that far off the mark. I have been single, more than not, in the last 24 plus years.

When my sister, Val, introduced me to a friend of hers, the friend asked how long I had been a single mom. Val immediately responded with, "always!" Then her friend asked me, "what is your type?" Before I could respond, Val quipped, "an asshole." Well then. That about sums that up! Yowza! Is that how people see me? My picker is broken! You have to listen to what people say and pay attention to what they do to learn from them! Just in case they are correct! WISE.

I was reminded of when I went to college, right out of high school, and how the girls in my dorm would talk about their dream guys and what they would look like. There would be ten or twelve fresh-man girls sitting around talking.

"He has a hairy chest."

"Oooh, not me! I don't want a hairy guy!"

"I want a tall guy, like a basketball player, so I feel small!"

"I want a guy to put his arm around my shoulders and I fit right inside perfectly!"

"My guy will have a nice tush!"

I am listening to them, yet not responding as I have never looked at a guy's 'tush' in my life! I care more about how smart he is, can he carry on an intelligent conversation. Is he a good tipper, appreciating what others do for him? Does he laugh at my jokes? Is he a man of God, good and fun? Does he continue to learn, reading books and such? Balance. I am looking for what I have not had in life, balance.

I wanted a man who was wise and open to learning. Sweet and strong. Someone more like me. **ADULTING**.

Perhaps it would have been easier all these single years if I had not compared the men I met to my sons, yet there you have it. I would choose someone more like them to be my partner. Someone smart, thoughtful, active, interesting who does not think I am crazy for having nine children. For a start…

I met the boys in Jason's hospital room on the morning of day three of Jason's accident and knew they needed to get to work. I hugged them and thanked them for being there for their brother and for me and told them I would call them if there was any reason to, but they could feel confident to get after their lives as best they could. I would stay with their brother. **RESPONSIBLE**.

When the hospital staff was not messing about with Jason and their machines, and it was just him and I in the room, I remembered what Kori had said about how acute his hearing would be, so I told him stories and had one-sided conversations.

Interestingly enough, a couple of weeks before his accident, he called me one Sunday, to ask if his kids could come and stay with us, for a while in Utah, which I agreed to immediately. He and the kid's mom were divorced, and they were both struggling financially, so they thought if they didn't have to pay for daycare for a little bit, or food for their toddlers, it would help the both of them get back on their feet a little bit. The kids and I were doing okay financially, so I felt I could handle that for a while. And my youngest were barely older than Jason's so they would like to play together. I made a quick trip to Tucson, up and back, to get Alyssa and Quentin, and the kids were happy to have time together in Utah.

I don't know what kind of work my grandkids mother, Lisa, was doing at the time, but Jason worked construction. And he was a diligent worker. In Tucson, construction workers get up at 0 dark 30 to beat the heat. Especially if they were working on a roof, which I believe he was at the time. Whether the neighbors liked it or not, they would be putting roofs on at 5 o'clock in the morning, or 6 o'clock in the morning, until the heat of the day got to them. Then they would do something else the rest of the workday, inside of an air-conditioned building preferably.

After his accident, it took a few days, for me to put together some of the pieces of the puzzle, of what happened to him, exactly. Jason rode a bullet bike, but he always wore a helmet, carried a backpack with books and things like that, and his water bottle. He always had his wallet with him.

He was headed home after work, when a woman driving a Lincoln, into the June Tucson sun, southbound at an intersection, turned right into his lane. He had no time to react and had no bruising on his hands from squeezing the brakes. With no wallet, backpack, or helmet, he went face first into the side of her Lincoln.

I'm going to interject in here that I had left my childhood religion years before this and subsequently taught my kids, "the fastest way to lose your spirituality is organized religion." Which I absolutely believed after my experiences in that church.

I also had lost my faith in any power bigger than me, with one thing after another making my life hard and often miserable. The behavior of others, losing everything I owned in a house fire, the death of my mother, the dissolving of my marriage, the harshness of poverty, the incessant sexual-harassment I dealt with in my job, and the instability of being a single parent, I found myself telling people, "My life has never been a picnic," as my attempt at a humorous reaction to my life.

I didn't think about God. I stopped studying scripture. I didn't feel like there was anything out there helping me get through my life. And then my oldest son almost lost his life, and the miracles started to unfold in front of my face.

The brothers left for work, and I was alone in the hospital room with Jason. With Kori's advice in mind, I was standing on one side of Jason's hospital bed when the resident doctor came in.

He was tall and handsome, with a very serious face and he told me, "Even after our best efforts, his prognosis is still death." Jesus. Ya know, sometimes when people say, 'Jesus' in reaction to something in life, it is not swearing. It is a prayer.

I put both of my hands on my hips, looked up into his face, and said, "you don't know Jason and if he wants to go, he's going to go. But if he wants to stay, he's going to stay, and he's gonna hold you accountable when he comes to, for everything you did or did not do for his best interests."

The doctor turned and left the room.

I was shaken. I was shaken, definitely by the doctor's words, and also by my reaction, because it didn't feel like it came just from me, but rather through me.

I grabbed my purse, hurried down the corridor through the locked doors, down another corridor to the elevators, down the elevator five flights, through the lobby, and out the doors.

Then started sobbing.

I hoped Jason couldn't hear me that far away. There was a patient drop off driveway in front of the hospital and I crossed it to a lovely little garden area, where people could sit on benches or walk around a path.

I took advantage of this several times a day, every day I was there. I paced and did not really see the flowers I was looking at. I must have been rough with the beaded bracelet I was wearing because I broke it, all over the walkway. I stopped walking to watch the beads bounce and roll in every direction.

Normally I would have gotten down on my knees to gather beads up to remake the bracelet, but I did not. The normally neat and tidy conservationist let the beads lay where they landed.

Every time I came to this little garden area after that, I would see my beads and be distracted by them. I suppose it is possible if you visited this place, if the garden is still there, you might be able to find an odd bead.

Death. That doctor said Jason's prognosis was death. Bullshit! I knew he was still here on the inside. I knew it was up to Jason whether he stayed or went. I pulled tissues out of a Ziploc bag I had packed full of them, blew my nose, pulled myself together and went back into the hospital, to fill another day of hanging out with my son in his coma. **PERSEVERANCE**.

CHAPTER 10

KID DREAMS

*It is when you are on a healing journey for your
own life, and that of your ancestors, you can
expect resistance from your family of origin and/
or the family you gave birth to, as they may not
be ready for the consequences of your healing, and
actually feel threatened. This is not a reason to
stop your healing journey.*

It is when you are on a healing journey for your own life, and that of your ancestors, you can expect resistance from your family of origin and/or the family you gave birth to, as they may not be ready for the consequences of your healing, and actually feel threatened. This is not a reason to stop your healing journey.

The only thing I really wanted when I was a kid, was to be married, have children, and take care of our family home. Well, I had the children. And I raised them to be independent, risk takers who go after what they want and do it well. They know how to find answers. Mission accomplished. So now what? All nine of my children are married or in long-term relationships. Most of them have children. Two of my sons married women with children, so over a year ago, I got an instant, four grandkid infusion! That was neat!

When my number four child, Stephan, was a young teen, he told me, "When I grow up, I'm going to marry a woman who already has children and be the best stepdad ever." That sure touched my single mom heart, hearing it from one of my sons. And he is one of the ones who married a woman with two beautiful redheaded daughters, to whom he is devoted. Warms the cockles of my heart. **COMPASSIONATE**.

It was never my intent to go through life alone and yet being single does have a lot of advantages from this perspective.

- You cannot get cheated on if you are not in a relationship.
- You do not have to ask permission to do anything.
- You can double dip your fries in Fry Sauce.
- And when you are on a road trip, and something catches your fancy, you can pull over to go check it out, without getting a lecture about somebody else's timetable.

Now the only thing holding me back from doing whatever I want is a tight budget! **WISE**.

Everybody has a budget of some kind, yet mine got really tight last year, when my biggest client did not renew my contract for another year, which I did not see coming. I had poured so much of my heart and soul into that position it took me nine months to realize that I felt like I had gone through a divorce. It literally caused me to grieve. And some of the subsequent bad behavior I had to deal with from some of them, finally brought me to a point, where I could emotionally walk away, and not care. But that took quite a lot as I do not quit easily. **TOLERANT**.

With that position, I had taken a situation which was disastrous, no matter how you look at it, and turned it around in a couple of years. It became a premier professional association, in this country. This non-profit went from 31 members to 369-ish and from allegedly $30,000 in the bank to well over 3/4 of a million dollars in the bank accounts. They went from five sponsors to 15, and between sponsors, strategic partners, and preferred vendors, they had a hundred companies providing various types of support, income to the association and member benefits. **FOCUS**.

Plus, the membership, themselves, had a noticeable increased love for their profession and their professional association in the State of Utah. Members would show up to events and socialize. They were happier to be there, which was a complete turnaround from when I handled my first event for them. I believe they knew I was their best ally in the state and truly cared about them and their work.

I am proud of the work I did for them. I was channeling my father and his love for his profession and the other members of my family, of four generations. My great grandmother, my grandfather, dad, my brothers, a brother-in-law, and others in my family had created a legacy I continued in that position. No matter what was said to discredit any of us, those in the know, knew who we were, and God knows the intent of our hearts. **HONOR**.

I had to come to the place of realization, I had let the behavior of a few break my heart and sour my desire for any further contact. The new kid on the job needed training, which the board apparently did not want me to provide. At her request, I helped her anyway. It was the right thing to do. And now I am in a place where I can emotionally let them go, as they let me go, last summer. **COMPASSIONATE**.

The bad behavior of other people affecting us, is a tough one to circumnavigate. When people lie and gossip about you it's a tough one to take. We want to fire back, or at least defend ourselves, and yet sometimes there is absolutely no point to it. One day, I heard from five different doctors complaining what had been said about me. I nearly called their general counsel or my own attorney. I was fed up with bad behavior. I paused. CALM.

Sometimes it is better to give no energy to the negativity of others. I waited until my daughter, Tegan, got home from work to tell her what was happening and get her take. Tegan's job title is very long as she is responsible for talent acquisition and training for a large national hospice corporation. She deals with this crap daily in one way or another.

She asked me, "have they accused you of anything illegal?"

"No."

"Then let it go. When someone leaves a company, it is human nature to blame everything that goes wrong after that, on the person who left, whether they deserve it or not."

"Well, that is pretty low behavior and unjustified. I do not appreciate being treated like this for no damn reason."

"I understand," she responded, "and yet there you are."

She gave me clarity and I took no action. 'Let them go and move on,' I thought. 'They are no longer your people,' I thought to myself. And I finally felt better. I paused until I had clarity, then took action, which in this case was no action. I felt freer, which was well worth it. **CALM**.

Lots of sayings went through my mind that day. 'Not my monkeys. Not my circus.' and more. Helen Mirren saying the advice she would give her younger self was to tell more people to, 'feck off' sooner. Not my way of handling things, yet I thought about it. My level of professionalism was higher than that. I saved it for this book! Just for you! **COMPASSIONATE**.

Sometimes it is the better part of valor to walk away. You know who you are. God knows who you are. And the people who really matter know who you are. So, everyone else can go stew in their own juices while you heal and move forward in a better direction for you. Pausing before you say anything or react, truly is a super-power.

Try it! It will blow people away, as few people can pull it off. However, if you make it your own practice, you will clearly see the wisdom in pausing first, then observing what your new superpower affords you! **RESOURCEFUL**.

CHAPTER 11

GOING PLACES

*And the pain you were going through during hard
times and the lessons you can learn from them
will become your strength and blessings in the long
run. Just so you know, this is your life. Yours. You
get to make your life choices. You also get all the
consequences of said choices. That's how it works!*

A nd the pain you were going through during hard times and the lessons you can learn from them will become your strength and blessings in the long run. Just so you know, this is your life. Yours. You get to make your life choices. You also get all the consequences of said choices. That's how it works!

I have always loved maps. I remember the big ones the teacher would pull down covering the chalkboard, because that is how old I am. When I was in school, we had chalkboards not whiteboards! Anywho, I loved the relief maps where you could see the altitude difference between mountains and lakes and things. And when Google Earth was invented, I was entirely fascinated by all the things I could look up. And so surprised at the things I could learn when I could actually see mountains under the ocean, and rugged terrain in the planet. **CURIOUS**.

I played with various types of GPS systems on cell phones and especially liked changing the voices. I always thought it would be fun to be the voice on a GPS. "No, your other right." "Well, let's just refigure your journey since you refuse to turn when I tell you to." I currently have the voice of a British Indian man which cracks me up. He is telling me where to go with a beautiful accent! **PLAYFUL**.

Although I was born in Chicago and grew up in the southern burbs of that great city, I have loved living in the mountains of the United States for most of my adult life. Colorado, Arizona, Nevada, Utah, Oregon, and California. They all have mountains and I have lived in them.

When people from flat states come to visit us, it can be quite the challenge for them to navigate the roads. Mountain roads do not just go straight up a mountain and then down. They have what are called switchbacks, where you snake your way up a mountain, back and forth, climbing higher and higher. Then repeating the process coming down the other side, pumping, NOT riding your brakes! That mountain driving tip is gratis. You will burn out your brakes, stink up the canyons and even overheat your motor if you do not drive correctly in the mountains.

Sometimes these are very narrow roads, with no barricades to keep you from falling off and they go on for miles and miles. My publisher shared the story of driving an older 35-foot Class A Winnebago Brave RV like this downhill for 57 miles on a road called Soldier's Summit. "We kept going up and up and I told my partner, this can't be good. What goes up, must come down," she told me. With trucks and RV's and even cars, sometimes, you have to learn when to downshift instead of using the brakes. Talk about scary, especially if you're a novice. These roads can be brutal! And very dangerous if you are not careful. Locals feel for the flatlanders here. **EMPATHY**.

As I write this, I live at just under 5,000 feet altitude. When I cross Salt Lake Valley my ears often pop, traveling in both directions, of course! And I have been in some horrendous driving situations living in the west, not only because of mountainous terrain, but the added horror of winter storms and blizzards.

A few years ago, my friend Sean invited me to come stay on his sailboat, in San Diego, when he was going to be out of town, for a while. I packed some bags to head in that direction. Swimsuits, a towel, minimal make-up, I do not wear much anyway and a few other items. Before leaving, I checked the weather only to see I would have to deal with a winter storm in southern Utah, right over the part of I-15 I hate to drive through snowstorms due to the added danger. **RESPONSIBLE**.

So, I looked at a map on my computer and thought I would just take a different route. My genius idea was, instead of going through Las Vegas, I would go through Eastern Utah, into Arizona to visit with my friend, Kathy, in Arizona City first. That would be fun, and then I could take I-10 from Phoenix to San Diego.

To get from where I was to the eastern part of Utah, I knew I could take I-15 to I-70 as these were good highways and well-maintained. But then I noticed a highway 6 which would cut through in only 50 miles from Spanish Fork to drop into Price, Utah. Score! Shave some time, whip down that way, and beat that storm!

I was up in the night!

Having never taken that route, and since it didn't look very big on the map, I thought this would be a great way to avoid that winter storm, get on the other side of the mountains, and head down to Moab from there. Boy was I wrong.

You would think a woman who had lived in the mountains most of her life would have done a little more checking about that route. I could see it was open when I plugged it into my GPS. There was no notice saying, 'closed for the season,' like many mountain roads are. So, with my packed Chevy Impala, I headed south to Spanish fork and then East on Highway 6.

Let me just say, by the time I got through that little 50-mile stretch, which looked so small on my map, my hands were exhausted from gripping the wheel! That route was full of semi-truck drivers going both directions. It had snowed quite a lot and the dirt from the semis and the road, mixed with the thick snow on the road, was like driving through cappuccino ice cream, in a boat. Rounding the curves in mountainous driving, or life in general, takes tremendous concentration and the development of critical skills. I am doing both and you can, too. **ADULTING**.

What had I been thinking? Mountain roads, winter weather, switchbacks, and big semi-trucks everywhere. These conditions require knowing how to focus, drive defensively and patiently round the curves. My allegedly genius idea could have gotten me injured or killed or worse. I might have hurt an innocent stranger. **HUMBLE**.

Flatlanders, as the locals affectionately call them, go off the road in the mountains every year. When I was a news director in radio on KVEL-News Talk Sports, I do not know how many stories I did about this.

One week, there were three semis which had gone off the road between Rock Springs, Wyoming and Vernal, Utah. It was almost as if the flatlander drivers made it so far and thought they had it made, only to fly off the road, just north of Vernal consistently. These roads are treacherous even in good weather. Add bad weather and they are nightmarish. Curve after curve, gaining in altitude or sometimes worse, going downhill, are brutal. People ride their brakes and burn them out until they smoke, shred, and become useless over time. You get the point.

At least I had new tires, but that did not change the fact, my trip down highway 6 might have been one of the dumbest decisions I had ever made in my life. That road twisted and turned, going up and down and up and down, while making its way through a small mountain range to drop into the valley housing Price, Utah.

I had to stop, rest my eyes, hands, and shoulders, and get something to eat. I pulled over in a McDonald's parking lot… to use my GPS, to find a better restaurant, of course.

I thought a cute little diner would be nice, so I did a search for a healthy restaurant and got bupkis. Then I just did a search for restaurants and got McDonald's and Taco Bell and places like that. While I was screwing around trying to find a place to eat, snowflakes started falling on my windshield and I thought, 'for crying out loud I don't seem to be avoiding this winter storm at all!'

So, I got back on the highway, headed to Moab. I figured it was probably a good hour and a half plus drive, but at least Moab has microbreweries and good restaurants! Moab Brewery Black Raven Oatmeal Stout, shrimp tacos, good night's sleep and the next morning I felt refreshed and rested. A quick stop at the Moab Coffee Roasters for a 16-ounce oat milk latte, kid temp and I was back on the road.

When life keeps throwing obstacles your way, keep going. They are not going to let up so do not let them get the best of you. **PERSEVERANCE**.

CHAPTER 12

A BROKEN FAMILY

*Give your energy to those who are trying to under-
stand and support you. Those who are absolutely
determined to hurt you through misunderstanding
and other methods, give them your silence and
zero energy.*

Give your energy to those who are trying to understand and support you. Those who are absolutely determined to hurt you through misunderstanding and other methods, give them your silence and zero energy.

I've shared stories from years ago with you here and lessons learned and tools I still use in my life. I have been through quite a lot in my life. I mentioned I tend to tell people my life has never been a picnic, which is a supreme understatement. For years, I felt 1998 was the worst year of my life. Losing my home and all of our possessions, dealing with the aftermath of a house fire, with all of my children, and their father, then losing my mother were just too much. But that was just spring of that year. **PERSEVERANCE**.

By fall, I was also divorced, and by January, my kids' father moved to Tucson, taking my five oldest kids with him.

Splitting up my family like that was devastating, particularly after all the other losses of that year. I had my four youngest living with me, and shortly after the split, the next two youngest came back. Their father could not register them for school, so he sent them back to me to finish that school year.

At this point, I had six children living with me in a two-bedroom home. My intent was to put my girls in one room with me, and all the boys in the other room with a couple of sets of bunk beds. I was outvoted. My kids had lost everything they owned, had an angry father, and zoned out mother. And they were kids. Where was their security? It was on me to provide it. **RESPONSIBLE. WISE**.

My two youngest boys liked sleeping at opposite ends of the same bottom bunk. So, Alex got the top bunk. But the girls did not want to be away from their brothers, so Danica's crib was in one corner and Tegan's single bed against the other wall.

Stephan slept on the pull-out couch in the living room and kept his clothes on shelves in the pantry.

I slept on the floor, (Why didn't you have a bed?) alone, in the other bedroom, since all the household stuff I got from the divorce was a slotted kitchen spoon and the kids beds. I cried when I was in the shower at night, hoping the kids couldn't hear me.

I missed my older sons and was often overwhelmed by how hard everything was. Not that my life wasn't hard before divorce, because that's why I got one! It was just a different kind of hard and sometimes life is like that.

We make decisions and every decision has new challenges. I came to a place where I would think about what the challenges would be, then made decisions, accepting the challenges as part of the changes in my life. RESPONSIBLE.

To help me cope and make the best decisions, I would periodically pause to do some exercise to gauge where I was in life, how I was handling things, and hopefully divine how I could improve.

I came up with a list of things I am good at doing. Some of my strengths I recognize:

- I can easily come up with simple solutions to complex problems
- I have a brilliant sense of humor
- Remaining calm in the middle of chaos is a strong habit now
- I am more generous than most people I know
- Understanding the feelings of others well is intuitive and a habit.

After the divorce, my children's father would never let the kids be together. He said I should have thought of that before getting divorced.

If it was my time with the older boys and his time with the younger kids, we were to switch kids, and I was to go on my way. He said, "your place is not big enough for all the kids and my place is not big enough for all the kids." I felt it was mean and spiteful and hurt the kids. That didn't matter to him. It took him moving to Tucson and my older sons getting their own apartment for me to be able to bring my younger kids to visit their brothers, sometime later.

Making road trips from Utah to Arizona was expensive, with my limited income, and tough with my job. I made 3 or 4 trips a year, on my dime. I have lots of stories about this time. The trips were an easy 14 hours and I drove straight through, only stopping for potty breaks and to get gas. I packed bananas, pretzels, and mozzarella sticks for snacking. Our 'go to' travel snacks! We stopped at fast food places for meals.

There were long stretches of road with no towns or houses or signs of man. As a lone woman traveling with all these little kids, I ran on faith. Faith we would be safe. Faith my Tundra would continue to run like a charm. **HOPEFUL**.

I could mention at this point, I divorced my children's father twice. That means we went through a divorce, then remarried after three months, when he promised so many promises. One of which was, 'if we get married again and you're not happy the next time, you can set up the divorce however you want. You can do whatever you want.' I didn't say anything in response, yet I did not believe him.

There was so much pressure from the community and the church we were members of at the time. People said things to me like, "How can you leave him when he's so down?" They had no idea what my kids and I were going through. He kept begging me to take him back. Promising he would keep a job, he would take care of us, we could work together to be able to buy our own home, and blah blah blah.

We got married on my birthday! That morning, I had taken my children to an obstacle course for us to have some fun and bond. I climbed a 3-story rope ladder then rappelled down the side. The kids did zip lines and flying fox swings and also some of them climbed the same structure I did. Josh even jumped from that structure to a three-story pole with a small metal platform on top. My kids were fearless. Even two-year-old Danica did a zipline with a pink safety helmet on! For some of the things my children were courageous enough to do, there's no amount of money you could pay me to try! **COURAGE**.

Within a month of our second marriage, my kids' father was back to his old ways. He was not helpful with the kids or around the house or property. He did not spend time with me or with the kids.

He groused around unhappy about everything. And I knew it was only a matter of time before he quit the most recent job.

I was still working and going to school at the same time. I knew somebody had to be responsible and attempt to build something better for the future of our family. **RESPONSIBLE**.

So many times, over the last decades, I've tried to remember our conversations about a second and final divorce and I cannot remember. One of my kids remembers us fighting and yelling. None of the other kids remember that. I do remember that time we were in our bedroom after getting the kids down for the night and my cell phone rang.

It was one of my clients who was coming out from Salt Lake to do a live radio remote the next day. He was just calling to verify details. He asked me if I was OK probably because he could hear something in my voice. I told him I was fine, and I would see him the next day and hung up.

As soon as I hung up my husband called me a "cunt," as if I were having an affair. Without a thought, I slapped him across the face.

I could not believe he called me something so disrespectful. I did not deserve it and was the mother of all of his children. I also could not believe I had just slapped the man I had loved since I was 17, the father of all my children. It was the final straw. **COURAGE**.

CHAPTER 13

PRETZELS & SHRIMP

*You own everything that happened to you. Tell
your stories. If people wanted you to write warmly
about them, they should've behaved better.*

—ANNE LAMOTT,
Bird by Bird: Some Instructions on Writing and Life

The final divorce went through in October of 1998, and in December, I got a $100 gift card to a grocery store from the radio station where I worked. Driving home to tell the kids about it, I thought about the day I moved them out of the house they were living in with their father.

I had spent the day moving their beds from their father's house we had shared, to the new one I had rented, then later putting their beds together. I had made trips to haul all their clothes and bedding, gotten their beds made, and their clothes put away in the closet. It didn't take long for me to move all of my clothes and some bedding because I had no bed myself, and no other furniture in the house.

Their father said, "take anything you think is yours." So, I took my kids, their beds, their things, my clothes. I had no furniture, no dishes, no pots and pans, no silverware, no food, of any kind. And somehow ended up with one large, slotted spoon. I don't know how! That was it.

So, after I got all of those things moved, I went back to the house to get the kids.

There is a black and white photo somewhere of my older kids bringing their younger siblings out to the car. Jason held Danica, the baby, and put her in her car seat. As the 1987 Honda Accord backed out of the driveway, with my four youngest children in their seat belts, I turned to drive down the road.

On the way to their new home, the conversation started. "Mom you should find somebody nice like Uncle Steve."

I held my breath.

"Now we can buy pretzels!"

"Now we can buy shrimp!"

"Now we can get Cheetos!"

I couldn't breathe. My kids, one after another, were talking about all the things they could do now that they weren't living with their father. I was so touched by the excitement in their voices and at such a young age. I saw this indication of how hard things had been on them, too.

"Now we can go to the reservoir."

"Now we can get Legos."

"Now we can get pets."

During all of this transition, Myke, an older man I sometimes worked with at the radio station, had become a dear friend. He took me on hikes showing me really cool places only older locals knew about. He told me story after story of the history of the Uintah Basin where we lived, taking my mind off of my troubles for a little while.

Later, when I got the kids down to bed, for the first night in their new place, I called to tell him about their conversation about pretzels, shrimp, and Cheetos. He was a wise and good listener.

The next day, after school, the house was abuzz with the activity of happy children, when the doorbell rang. It was Myke with bags of groceries! The kids lost their minds! The bags held Cheetos and pretzels, shrimp, and mozzarella sticks! And there was a bag with Legos and two baby dolls, so they now had toys!

It is very important, the rougher your life is, to have excellent friends. Friends who listen. Friends who are unselfish and truly care about your well-being. Myke and I could not be a couple because he was older and did not want to help raise children. I understood that. He had already done it in his life. But we could be friends, and a great one he was. **TEACHABLE**.

Over time, I realized how restricted I had been during my marriage regarding building friendships. I was busy with the kids and household, yet I did not have access to money, phone or a vehicle for some of the time. It is hard to build friends when you cannot go anywhere or have money for coffee or lunch.

I certainly had no one to discuss the problems in my marriage, as that was not done. Mom told me not to tell her if I had marriage problems. The few times I tried to speak with a church leader I was told things like, "your husband is homosexual." "You must stay with him so he can lift you up in the last day," to which I asked, "how can he lift me up when he lives in hell?" That did not land well. **HONOR**.

Let me insert something here which helped me and might help you, too. When things happen, it is human nature to want to tell somebody. We want a listening ear. Some sympathy, or better yet, empathy. But a terrible idea, is telling the wrong person. Figuring out who the right and wrong people are to share with, is a good thing to get good at quickly! **WISE**.

One of the best sources of information on this is anything spoken or written by Dr. Brene' Brown. If you do not know who she is, you are in for a treat! She is highly trained and experienced in character traits and navigating life and is down to earth enough to share her stories with us. Including her 'shame' stories.

She taught me two important concepts. One, never share your 'shame' stories with the wrong person. Brene Brown says shame cannot survive empathy. I take the risk of telling my 'shame' stories here with the intent they will help others. Whether they do or do not help you is up to you. I did my part! (Check the Resource pages in the back of the book.) **EMPATHY**.

Back to the gift card we got from the radio stations where I worked for Christmas. I thought in telling my kids about this largesse, they would want to buy all kinds of treats and fun things to eat from the grocery store. I was incorrect in that assumption.

"Let's get cookie sheets and measuring spoons and cups!"

"And flour and sugar and things to bake with!"

"Could we get a toaster Mom?"

"And maybe a mixer for mixing cake batter and brownie batter!"

"And we'll need racks to put the cookies on for cooling. Do we have enough money to get all these things, Mom?"

I had already bought bright red and blue plastic picnic plates and bowls, carefully hand washing them so they would last. Plastic picnic silverware was added and drinking cups. We used these for months, until I started looking for more solid dishes and glasses at a local thrift shop. Our kitchen things were a bit of a modge podge. I was explaining how I bought thrift store mismatched dishes and glasses to a friend who asked me if they were clean. "Of course, I washed them!"

"Then they match," she calmly replied! **WISE**.

Smiling, I was grateful for what I had. My kids were settling into their new lives, finding joy in little things, and so could I. I worried all the time for them. Worried my decision to get divorced would have lasting detrimental effects on them. I worried they were not happy, and I could not give them what two parent households could provide. **RESOURCEFUL**.

When their birthdays came around, I prepared a favorite meal with a cake or their favorite dessert, David's was strawberry shortcake! Then I planned a party, inviting their friends, generally serving hotdogs and banana Creamies. I could not afford gifts, yet I could create a party where friends could gift them. **RESPONSIBLE**.

We work with what we have got to work with, making the best of it and are grateful for it. Doing the best we can, with whatever we have to work with, is solid adulting there! Stepping away from judging and comparing how we are doing with anyone else is a wise idea. Give yourself grace. Be patient and be proud of yourself for what you get through and for how you are becoming a better, more understanding person for it. Take your lumps then learn from them. **GRACE**.

If that is not what you are doing, you can adjust. Any moment you can make new decisions, choosing a different way to live. I continually work on becoming a better version of myself. It is a big ass chore! I have a long way to go, yet I have made it this far, and intend to keep at it. Fortunately, I have found so many amazing mentors along the way. I like the woman I have become. In fact, If I weren't me, I would want me for a friend and that is a good place to be! **HAPPY**.

CHAPTER 14

FROM REPULSIVE TO NOT BAD

Do not steal, do not lie, do not be lazy.
—QUECHUA PROVERB

As a new divorcee in my early 40s, the first men showing me attention were unhappily married men. One asked me, "If I left my wife, would you marry me?" The fact that he was even asking me was enough to put me off. Why would I think he wouldn't do that to me if he were married to me? Cheaters cheat.

One of my married clients, after an hour and a quarter of negotiating his annual advertising contract asked me, "Now, can we have sex?" Knowing his office door was open and anyone in his office could have heard him, I quickly responded with, "You don't have enough time in your schedule for 1 minute!" And I took my contract and left. **WISE.**

His obnoxious brother ran a clothing store in town, and when I came into visit that client he said, "I'd like to see you in one of these new silk blouses on a cold day." I left his shop and told the station owner I would never call on him again so give that account to somebody else. Repulsive.

I had a blind date and all I can remember about him, at this point, was that whoever set us up told me he was a millionaire, and his home was paid for and when he picked me up, he had a nice car. So, as we were driving away from my house, I looked around the dashboard and what I could see of the car and asked him what kind of a car it was. Big mistake. Because I did not know what kind of car he was driving, he was no longer interested in me. But we had made plans for a double date to have dinner and watch a movie with another couple I knew, so the evening continued.

Dinner was lovely because the other couple were fun, interesting people, but my date said little. Of course, he didn't speak much during the movie and when we were leaving the theater saying good night to the other couple, I noticed he had already walked to his car, got in and had left me 5 miles from my house! I had to call my son to come and pick me up. It was a little awkward and part of me felt minimalized by that behavior. But the bigger part of me felt relief to not be involved with someone that shallow and mean. **TOLERANT. BOUNDARIED.**

Another thing I learned during this period of time was how many men depend on their wives for even the littlest of things. The internet was new, and I got on a dating website because clearly, I was not meeting anyone acceptable where I lived. I made arrangements to meet the CEO of a company from Park City at a restaurant in Heber City and quickly after meeting him became baffled. How could a man running a company not brush his teeth? And I mean, not brushing his teeth to the point they practically had fur on them. It was repulsive to sit across the table from someone I could see a coating on the outside of his teeth. Who did he think was going to want to kiss that mouth? Certainly not me! **ADULTING.**

That was a short lunch, wherein I tried not to think about him trying to kiss me and shuddering! We said goodbye in the parking lot and then, as I was getting in my truck, he hollered back at me, "Hey, so do the dry cleaner people bring your clothes to you?"

Oh, dear God! Did his wife do absolutely everything for him?

"Brush your teeth, honey."

"Here's your outfit for the day, dear."

"It's time to take a shower!" Oh, for heaven's sakes!

I had raised nine children. I had no intention of connecting with such a clueless man! Not my job to raise another big kid.

I've met men looking for a nurse or their mommy or someone just to look pretty on their arm. I've met men thinking I was loaded because I know how to dress and have class and manners. I had a guy tell me across the table from the first time we met, "I'm not going to put your children through college."

"Who asked you to?"

For heaven's sakes, what in the world is the matter with these guys? **BOUNDARIED**.

At some point, my brother, Derek, shared a parable with me which made me feel better. Derek said, "The best women are like the apples at the top of the tree, all kissed by the sun, perfectly ripe and flawless."

"That was nice! Go on!"

"Most men are content to pick an apple they can reach. Some men don't even mind picking up the half rotten ones off the ground. Ewee. It takes somebody special to plan ahead, bring a ladder, carefully set it up and then reach for one of the best apples at the top of the tree."

Well, there you go! Thank you, Derek! I still think of that, and it makes me feel better yet I'm still alone. **ADAPTABLE**.

I feel like inserting, "meanwhile, back at the ranch," periodically in this book! I know the stories are all over the place, yet isn't that how life is? My life is!

My sons visited Jason in ICU at the University of Arizona Medical Center when they got off work, so we missed each other as I had to pick up Ronnal, to return her car and get back to her place.

That night, the night nurse thought it was a good idea to tell my son, David, who was barely 20 at this point, his brother was going to die after I left the hospital the first day.

David was so upset. That was crushing to the younger brother.

I could not believe a professional would be such an ass. He got the full brunt of the Cross family the next day and was told never to come anywhere near Jason again. So, on day three of Jason's ordeal, we had an angelic nurse, whose name I no longer remember, I am sad to say.

She had been working as a traveling nurse for quite some time and would decide where she wanted to live and then go there, work as long as she wanted, until she thought of a different place she wanted to live. She told me she had been in Tucson for longer than she normally stayed in a place, and she had wondered why she didn't feel the need to leave yet.

When Jason came into the hospital, she had a different patient that night. She heard about him and wanted to be his nurse. So, she made sure she was his nurse for the next two days of her weekly shift and then she traded with somebody else so she could have him for the next three days after that for a total of five straight days.

She was a godsend literally, completely professional and compassionate. The staff started calling Jason the million-dollar patient.

Every day was a similar pattern. I would get to the hospital as soon as I dropped off Ronal at her job and spend time with my son and the hospital staff. When it was time to pick her up from work, I would say good night to Jason and spend time with my sons after they got off work.

I would also call home to talk to Alex to find out what was going on with the kids. My town rose up to help me. They took my kids for haircuts, to the swimming pool, to movies and all kinds of fun things. Nobody told the little kids what was going on in Tucson, including both of Jason's little kids, who were toddlers at the time. They just thought they were having the time of their lives.

It was tough on 16-year-old Alex because he really wanted to be in Tucson, but he kept track of where all of his siblings were and kept me updated. He had food for groceries and my Tundra to keep him busy. It was a tremendous responsibility for someone so young, and yet I could not have been there for Jason without Alex being so responsible. **ADULTING**.

CHAPTER 15

THE FIGHT IS ON

We are all visitors to this time, this place. We are just passing through. Our purpose here is to observe, to learn, to grow, to love ... and then we return home.

—ABORIGINAL AUSTRALIAN PROVERB

For Jason, I had purchased a book about living a simple life and enjoying things in the season. It was full of recipes and simple, fun things to do, depending on what season it was. I bought it so that I could read it in short little bites of information, which wouldn't trigger him assuming he could hear me.

I also got a journal so when people came to visit, they could write messages to Jason, for when he came out of his coma. There was also something about my twisted sense of humor, lack of patience, and how long he was still in a coma, because I started interjecting things, I thought he would balk at.

I borrowed a little boombox and played country music on it, especially the Dixie Chicks because he hated country music in his normal life. I pictured him snapping out of his coma telling me off to my delight. Except that didn't happen.

And I tried telling him how my salsa was better than his because I liked slivers of garlic for that yummy deliciousness when you get a big chunk in your mouth. And that was because when he made salsa, he would mince the garlic into tiny little bits and then stir it in. But that didn't make him come out of his coma either.

All of my kids like to cook and each of them have something they are especially good at making. And we all make our versions of fresh salsa.

Somewhere there's a picture of Jason at seven years old, standing on a chair in front of a stove, with a pancake on a spatula, looking under it to see if it's cooked. Impressive photo, wherever it is. I figured if I couldn't sweet talk him into coming out of his coma, I would piss him off so he would come out of it!

He shared an apartment with his brother, David, and he and I decided to go to their apartment to get some pictures of Jason to tape them up in his hospital room for the staff to see what he was supposed to look like when they're finished with him.

It was really hard for David to go to the apartment and not have Jason there. He had been doing that for a few nights at this point, and I hadn't realized. It made him emotional and sad, so in addition to photos of Jason, I grabbed a couple of pins he had that were funny. I can't remember what any of them said, but I know there were a couple of 'F' bombs involved.

David and I talked about what we would do if Jason needed long-term care, even for the rest of his life. He said the brothers could build a ramp at my house for a wheelchair. I said I would give up my room on the main floor or we would make his room in the living room so there was more room for a wheelchair. There was never any question I would take care of him as long as I could.

There was never a question his brothers would help me any way they could, even if they were 800 miles away. We had a plan for just in case, and both of us heaved big sighs of relief. We got a roll of scotch tape at Target, and the next day I decorated his hospital room with photos from his life.

I stuck the funny, yet possibly inappropriate, pins on the inside of his curtains, so they faced out the window and would not offend anybody. I could show people who I thought would think it was funny because they were Jason's sense of humor.

We pointed out the pictures to the staff when they would come in the room and told them this is what we're expecting them to return to us when they're through messing about.

There were pictures of his little kids, Quentin, and Alyssa, we affectionately called Q and A. And we told the staff they needed their dad back healthy and whole, ASAP.

It was such a difficult time. I know I was not in my right mind, yet I kept attempting to do the next right thing, wonky as my efforts might have been then. And I was very aware of not having a significant someone in my life to support me through this. I called to download my day to friends, yet I felt it was too much stress on them, and they did not know how to make me stop! **PERSISTENT**.

More recently, I saw a video on social media with Jordan Peterson and an unnamed woman. The woman talked about how smart women with an IQ of 145 or more are only going to connect with men of high IQ of 145 or more. And my immediate thought was, men that smart have already found somebody, and their partners are doing what needs to be done to keep them.

Then the woman said, men with an IQ of 135 or more don't care about the IQ of their woman, so they will choose women with low-er IQs because it doesn't matter to them. So smart women want smart men, yet smart men don't care. Hmmm, interesting. I suppose we could hypothesize all over the place on this one, yet perhaps I will just let the statistic sit there, for now.

I choose to believe that's why I'm single. Because I'm smart! And it makes me laugh! Even in the midst of struggle, something funny will pop up to lighten the heavy load in my brain. **HUMOR**.

Single or not, this is still your life, and you get to make your decisions, set your boundaries, and go after your goals. I hypothesize it might be easier with a supportive partner, and yet I've never had one, so I do not really know. From here it is simply a theory I may or may not ever get to test. It's okay. I have adapted. **ADAPTABLE**.

Coincidentally, I always told my children they should not take advice from someone who is not where you want to be. So, my relationship advice is a lot of what not to do because I know that stuff from personal experience! And yet I do read and study and have created theories I believe would work with the right partner, as I just mentioned.

I see no reason why you should ever fight for one thing. You can have a calm discussion even if you disagree. And if you have shared goals for your life together, you can make sure all decisions add to that and bring you closer to your goals. It just seems to me, over time, people grow in different directions, if they do not make a concerted effort to strengthen their relationship. This is true for all kinds of relationships though.

There's you, and there's the other guy or gal and then there's the relationship, which is a living growing thing, if you do it right. And that relationship has to take a high priority and be purposefully nurtured. Otherwise, it will not stand the test of time. This is something I do know well from personal experience. **COOPERATIVE**.

Now I do have friendships I have practiced my theories on, and they work! I have friendships I've had for 25 or 30 plus years because we love each other, care about each other, support each other, and we stay in touch.

Monday mornings at 9:00 tends to be coffee with my friend, Richard, if possible. We used to go to coffee together every two weeks when he would be out in Vernal, Utah, for his job. When I moved to Salt Lake City, there was a group of his friends I would meet with on Sunday mornings at Badass Coffee Shop on State Street.

Over time, I didn't like meeting with this group because the other men always talked about war and weapons and that got old. They weren't even swapping stories of when they served in the military because none of them did. They just liked to collect information about different kinds of guns and talk about it. And the other women that we used to meet with moved out of the area or stopped coming and I did not want to be the only woman there listening to conversations I'd rather not hear. **BOUNDARIED**.

So, Richard and I started meeting for coffee once or twice a month trying different coffee shops, which was fun. I discovered I was his only positive friend. All of his stories were a little bizarre about the things other people thought and did. Without a job currently, I have had the time to meet with him more often, and it has been quite enjoyable. In all these years we have been friends meeting at various coffee shops, I have only met his wife once. Yet I know all about her, their kids, grandkids and Richard's friends and his adventures with his jobs and golf and all kinds of other things. You have got to have things you do for the fun of it. Let joy in! **PLAYFUL**.

Since meeting him, I worked on being a better listener. And I would collect interesting stories during my week to share with him when we got together. I don't suppose there is anything I could share with him that would surprise him. We share information about nutritional supplements we're trying and what's going on in the world, and he even gave me some golf lessons for a while last year. So, I know nurturing a friendship can make it last and be strong. My only fear is that something will happen to him, and I won't know about it because nobody will call me. But I'm not going to worry about that. I will just show up for coffee next week. Coffee with friends is something I do for my soul, and the conversations are intriguing. **CREATIVE**.

We have to have things which are creative. If all we do is work to solve problems, we burn out. I have done this several times in my life not knowing it's a thing! I had to be told by an employment counselor when living in Santa Cruz, California because I did not know it was a thing. I lumped it into depression. Depression is something I am quite familiar with since I was growing up. Mom suffered from it. She used sleep to comfort herself. No one called it depression back then. Dad may not have even known about it, away at work all day.

CHAPTER 16

AN EDUCATION

The roots of all things are holding hands. When they cut down a tree in the jungle, a star falls from the sky.

—LACANDÓN PROVERB

When I got home from school, Mom would take whoever the baby was at the time, close the door to her bedroom and I was in charge of all the kids. I changed diapers, handled whatever came up, made dinner, fed everyone, and then got them ready for bed.

Mom would come out of her room, five hours later, freshened up, put a pot of water on to boil with cinnamon or herbs in it to give the illusion dinner was cooking for my dad when he walked through the door. He went in their room to shower and change out of his suit and when he emerged, dinner was ready for him.

We never ate the same thing Mom and Dad did for dinner. I only know how to boil pasta, open cans, and make up something. They had grilled fish, steaks, and all kinds of recipe deliciousness Mom would find in magazines. I learned adults were more valuable than kids, one of my many limiting beliefs.

After they ate, I would clean up those messes, pull out the iron, ironing board, starch and water spray bottle to iron Dad's shirt and trousers for the next day.

Once we had a babysitter who tried to iron Dad's clothes instead of me. She burned a tie and left a burn mark on his dress shirt. When my parents came home and saw it, I got grounded. I, a junior high kid, should not have let an adult do my chore.

One time in the summer, when days were longer, Dad came home when it was still light out. Light and sticky hot in the humid Chicagoland air. We decided to run through the sprinkler and were having such fun! Running and jumping over the water, laughing, and taunting each other, when my father grabbed my upper arm, hurt me and yelled at me. I had no idea what I had done wrong. His angry face was close to mine when he yelled at me to go in the house and change my wet clothes.

Why did he yell at me? Why was I singled out and removed from the fun? I did not understand. At 12 years of age, in a white button-up shirt, the sprinkler water had created a wet t-shirt effect on my young developing body. Why anger was Dad's response is on him. I did not know. No one had talked to me about wearing bras. I was an innocent child abruptly moved out of the circle for being a girl.

Later, Mom bought me a beginner's bra. Being a girl became a limiting belief that I did not recognize until going through David Bayer's programs identifying limiting beliefs to change them. WISE.

Another limiting belief I developed at a young age was that my only value was while I was working, doing chores, schoolwork, helping my mother, or taking care of siblings. Production meant value. I had to hide reading books. If Mom caught me reading a book, she gave me a chore to do. There was no end of chores in a big family.

Being a voracious reader from an early age, I read everything in front of me. The entire cereal box, Parade magazine, the comics, books from the library, and even Dad's college textbooks!

I read Dad's college chemistry book when I was 12 and memorized the table of elements. As a born philomath, that is understandable, plus I was always looking for Dad's approval. The one thing he complimented me on was my intellect, so I learned things to share with him when I could get his attention. **PERSISTENT**.

He asked what I wanted to be when I grew up. I wanted to be a wife and a mother and take care of our home. I told him, "I either want to be a chemical engineer or do what you do."

"You want to be a doctor?"

"No. I want to travel and lecture!"

"What topic do you want to lecture on then?"

"It doesn't matter. I just want to help people." He turned and walked away.

A 12-year-olds perspective was too rudimentary for him, I assumed. It was so hard to understand what I had to do to be important, besides being a worker drone, to the important people in my life. I had questions I couldn't voice. I was continually confused at home whenever I even had time to think about it.

If I had known what to ask, it might have been, 'What builds resilience?' If I had had a clue what my life would look like and entail, I would have prepared better for it. Resilience. Being able to move through life's challenges smoothly. How could I have prepared myself? Strong meaningful relationships with others who care deeply about you are an excellent method. I know this now. I surely did not then. Nor when I was in college. Nor as a young mom. Nor even as an older mom. It took a lifetime of effort and mindful focus to get here, and it's not perfect. Being able to learn from others is the only shortcut I know to get places. Learn from my experiences and save yourself! Strengthen your character to be resilient. You will be happier. I pinkie promise. This also results in fewer depressive symptoms and more well-being as we get older.

It is especially important for children to get this support from a young age. And this does not mean do everything for your kids. It means teach them how to do things themselves, so they are empowered and can navigate life themselves. Accomplishing things on their own is its own reward and quite satisfying.

Mentors are a great resource for building character and strength in easier ways. Listen with an ear to applying their wisdom to your own life. Then, do the recommended exercises in lieu of getting kicked by life to learn. I have been blessed with a plethora of really cool mentors, coaches and counselors, and I have learned from all of them. (Check out the Resource pages in the back of this book.)

Find people you can be inspired by who care about you. Create your own family of support. Get strong and be resilient, then whatever comes, you don't lose your way. **RESOURCEFUL**.

Before I went through my divorce, I qualified for a federal program to help me get the education I needed to thrive in the workplace. It required evaluation by a psychologist who diagnosed me with major recurrent depression. Big surprise.

It meant this government program would pay for my college education. All of it. So, when I qualified for grants and student loans, I could use those to help support my kids and me. I had to meet with the psychologist routinely, which I found terribly interesting because of all the things I learned about him in our chats.

He had a fascination for conversations with psychopaths and sociopaths, so he had interviewed many of the murderers in the Utah prison system. Not my normal topic of conversation with anyone else. Why my counseling sessions were generally him talking about his shizz is probably because I was such a good listener! And to be in the program, I had to have counseling appointments, so there ya go. I did what I had to do. **WISE**.

Sometimes you don't know the right thing to do, so you keep doing what you are doing until something makes you look at it with a fresh perspective.

It was somewhere between the third and the fifth day after Jason's motorcycle accident, when I had a visit from an EMT who had responded to Jason's accident. I was eager to meet him, to not only thank him, but to listen to his version of what had happened.

One of Jason's nurses had told me that he had to be resuscitated at the scene. The EMT said that didn't happen, in fact, quite the opposite!

Tell me this isn't a miracle … On the scene when this accident happened were three professionals on their days off! This EMT was one of them! I assumed he had responded to the call but nope, he and another EMT and a police officer, were all there when it happened!

He said they all left their vehicles to run to the scene to immediately to start care. I'm still in awe of this miracle of timing!

The EMT said Jason fought all of them, and they were all covered with his blood! He obviously had trauma, could not see out of either of his eyes, was bleeding from his head, face, and knee, which had hit something on the handlebars going over the front of his bike. For his own safety, they were trying to restrain him until the ambulance got there and then they had to restrain him because he was not okay in the head and was fighting everybody!

Then, when he got to the emergency room, they gave him plasma, and he went into anaphylactic shock. So, they had to deal with that, however it is that you deal with that.

By the time I got to the hospital the next day, there had been seven different things that had happened, which Jason could have died from, only he didn't.

They had filled him full of fluids to the point that he weighed 200 pounds, which is a significant weight gain for a fit, young construction worker. All of his nutrition was going into his body via tubes and IVs. And I was not the only one noticing that both the right and left sides of his brain were showing more activity every day. I found that very hopeful. **HOPEFUL**.

At this point, the strain was taking a toll on me and on the seventh day, I left the hospital for the garden area and sobbed my guts out. I cried out, looking at the sky and said, "You must fix this! This is too big for me, and I can't do it. You have to fix this. He has two young children who need him. Their mother is nuts, and you can't leave them with her. I have four little kids of my own and no help. I don't know how I would take care of an invalid adult son on top of it. But if I need to I will. You must help me now!"

I wasn't sure who I was talking to but if anybody was listening, they needed to step it up and help. I could not deny the miracles I was seeing in Jason's life, and my faith was coming back.

"You have to fix this!" became my version of prayer at the time. I've heard intelligent people often have a habit of talking to themselves, and I believe humble people talk to a power bigger than themselves. **SPIRITUAL**.

CHAPTER 17

KEEP LEARNING

My language is my awakening, my language is the
window to my soul.

—MĀORI PROVERB

On day eight I went to visit Jason in the hospital, and they would not let me in his room because they said they had some things to do, whatever that meant. So, I went to the downstairs lobby to wait. I was sitting on a vinyl-covered chair against the wall when an older woman came and sat down by me. She was all kinds of beside herself with excitement because her husband was in getting his annual bank of tests done. She said he had been a heart recipient six years earlier and was doing so well he just had to come in once a year for checkups.

She told me they belong to a support group of people who had been recipients of organs, and there were also people in the group anticipating receiving an organ, at some point, to save their lives.

She told me springtime was the best time of the year because that's when people started riding their motorcycles and getting in wrecks, so organs became available. Yep, she told me that. To my face. And I listened. **WISE**.

I've shared this story with people through the years who are generally baffled with the fact that I did not tell her why I was in the hospital. It never occurred to her to ask me. And I could mention, while I was in the hospital with my son, after his motorcycle accident, that six other men had been brought into the University of Arizona Medical Center due to motorcycle accidents and only one of them had lived. He lived because he smashed his leg and did not hit his head, miraculously. I had learned that from the nurses coming to take care of my son every day. **TOLERANT**.

So no, she did not ask why I was in the hospital, and I did not tell her. I patiently listened to her excitement over her husband's healing, and I was happy for them. I know. I am not normal. **COMPASSIONATE**.

This compulsion I had to find answers to why I was so different so I could fix it was something I was driven to do for decades. Reading a wide variety of self-help books was something I started when I was pregnant with my oldest son Jason. So, before I even started having children and raising them, I was trying to learn how to be a better person.

Psychologist visits lasted for the length of time I was going to Utah State University, Vernal and Roosevelt campuses, until I moved to Salt Lake City in December 2003. The psychologist ran all kinds of tests on me including Intelligent Quotient and Myers-Briggs. He said I was an INFJ or an INTJ depending. My personality type apparently hit about in the middle of "T" and "F." He recommended I do some research on Myers/Briggs to see what I thought about it. I thought I would see how I felt about it, which was a good indication I was more 'Feeler' than 'Thinker' when making decisions. Whatever related topics I came across, I would read every book in the library on said topic.

I read every book by Wayne Dyer, Deepak Chopra, Louise Hay, reading topics about dream interpretation, hypnosis, therapies from homeopathies to Reiki to quantum physics. My interests were all over the place, but always trying to understand who I was, so I could be better. **CURIOUS**.

The library had a limit on how many books I could check out at one time, so I got library cards for all my kids. I encouraged them to check out books and videos. The rule was more books than videos. They negotiated among themselves even trying to get the younger ones to check out more videos.

Those little guys already saw the value of the beautiful art and interesting stories in picture books, so they did not cave. I assigned each older kid to read to younger kids every day. It is challenging to manage 9 kids or even smaller numbers of them. Eventually, I figured out one of the older boys, Stephan, (pronounced Stefan) was 'reading' the same book every day. Chatty Chipmunks Nutty Day or something like unto it. I put 'reading' in quotes as he was simply telling the story as fast as possible to go do something else. Punk! I gave birth to punks! **HUMOR**.

That also surfaced in his late teens as he struggled with spelling. I was sorry that I did not catch it earlier, yet pleased he came to me for help. His job required daily reports so he would call me and ask how to spell things sometimes, after the younger ones were asleep. I was happy to help, and now he owns his own successful business, decades later, yet I digress.

Back to the search for why I was different and what I did to find out. I checked out books from the library on astrology and then discovered Chinese astrology and found I could put the two of them together for some really interesting conversations with people.

My signs are Aquarius and Goat. I read I was an iconoclast and had to look it up. It means if something has always been done a certain way, I have a compulsion to destroy it so something more correct can be built in its place. I liked that. I believed if something can be destroyed by truth, it should be. **HONEST**.

I also read my Wood Goat sign in Chinese astrology was "a shored-up and buttressed Goat person … most likely to be able to surmount harsh setbacks and carry on valiantly as though nothing untoward had occurred." Well, hell. I was rather tired of harsh setbacks and acting like nothing was wrong! **EMPATHY**.

I studied crystals and philosophies, religions, and history. I was fascinated by the beautiful coffee table books with art and photography. I read every book I could find written by Agatha Christie, Louis Lamour, Robert Ludlum, Tom Clancy, and so many other authors. Once I found an author I liked, I used the library to find every book they had ever written. Eventually, I would start buying books to build a library of nonfiction books I considered reference and some novels I liked to read more than once.

Even though I was not impressed with the recent Wrinkle in Time movie version, I had read that book many times since I was nine years old. I loved the interwoven plot lines and the things I learned about friendship and having a good character. Although I did not have a name or definition for it, I studied every quantum related thing I could find after reading a Wrinkle in Time. **PERSISTENT**.

In 1998, my friend, Margaret, used a computer program, to pull my entire natal chart with my birthday, time of birth and location of birth. She also pulled my husband's natal chart and a report putting the two charts together. I wanted to see what we looked like energetically. The marriage was ending anyway, yet I found it interesting it didn't even look like we ever should've connected in the first place, according to our astrological charts.

When I discovered Chinese astrology, putting our two signs together was actually the absolute worst relationship combination in all of Chinese astrology!

I still stuck it out for 23 years! **PERSEVERANCE**.

CHAPTER 18

IF I ONLY KNEW WHAT GOD KNOWS

Nobody can say he is settled anywhere forever: It is only the mountains which do not move from their places.

—MAASAI PROVERB

While the woman waiting for her husband at his 6th annual heart checkup was chatting away, two of the techs, who usually worked with Jason walked by and asked me why I was in the waiting room. I told them the staff would not let me in, and they asked, "Do you know what's going on?" and I said I didn't. They told me to come with them to his room.

I know I shared the story earlier in the book, but this is when the room was full of hospital staff, and I was standing at the foot of Jason's bed quietly watching them. He was trying to breathe on his own, which he had not had the strength to do before this. They had stopped giving him the coma-inducing drugs, and he was starting to come to.

They were asking him questions after taking the tube out of his throat. He was antsy and kept trying to pull his catheter out, which I understand is a terrible idea. However, I can understand it would also be annoying to have one in your body. He would try to mess with it, and I would pull his gown down.

His doctor asked him if he knew who I was. He could not see me because of the damage to his bandaged eyes. And we could tell he recognized something about my voice, but it was not connecting in his brain. This disturbed him, so I said, "I'm one of the helpers taking care of you," which calmed him down.

Since the staff had previously thought, he was not going to survive, they were not treating the dollar coin-sized wound on his knee. I had told them to bring me the stuff to take care of it, and I cleaned it, put ointment on it and bandaged it. I asked them for swabs to clean his mouth and teeth for him. **COMPASSIONATE**.

If you have not been around a head injury victim, you probably do not know the extraordinary odor it causes in their mouths. I have no idea why, but it is intense and memorable. He also had some odd scrapes on his forearms that I had cleaned and doctored myself. Then, I had the genius idea to get those melting strips for your breath and just stick them in his mouth when he was in his coma to improve his breath.

What I discovered was that he reacted to them in his coma and would try to get them off his tongue by making weird faces, while scraping his teeth across his tongue! It was highly entertaining to me, until I saw his teeth were broken and missing in the front and had cut his tongue.

Geez, Louise. I felt like such a bad mom. I also noticed his tongue ring piercing was gone and wondered where that went.

I was encouraged when he reacted to the breath strips. This gave me tremendous amounts of hope. I know we all needed hope at that point. Jason and his kids were depending on us. **HOPEFUL**.

It is unbelievable how difficult life is when you have no hope for the future. I had made a covenant with my children's father and God to be faithful in my marriage, and I had given it my best shot. All things considered, with who I was at the time, and what I had to work with, that was as good as it was going to get. Not good enough.

Both parties should be trying if you want it to work out. I came to the conclusion that things were never going to get better, and although I still loved my husband, I had also learned love is not enough. I needed to admire and respect my man, and I did not. I knew it would never work any better than it did right then, which again, was not good enough. **GRACE**.

Believing I would disappoint God, I could no longer stay in the marriage. I felt God would give me grace and let me out. I would focus on providing for my children.

I rationalized it this way; my kids deserved one parent trying, over two parents who were completely fucked up. I was well on the way to learning how to quit sugarcoating things and to call a spade a spade. Even if it was a mixed metaphor. **RESPONSIBLE**.

By 2003, I pulled my natal chart again, to see if another version would tell me anything new about myself or my potential in life. Both natal charts painted the picture of a hard life. Dammit. I was hoping something was going to improve. Yes, I looked at it from a different perspective. It still sucked. Such a recurring theme, to keep looking in whatever thing came along, for answers.

In 2014, I pulled another natal chart, like it was going to say something different one of these times!

In 2016, I discovered the Kolbe Index. A doctor recommended this for me, and I am sooooo grateful he did! I took it after 10 p.m. one night after running an event that day with hundreds of doctors. I was tired, headed to burnout, but I had $50 or whatever it cost, so I did it. Answered about 36 questions without thinking at all and BAM! I got a huge report in my email. I loved it!

It explained how different I am from lots of other people, especially the ones I was working with at the time. Where they needed lots and lots of information, details, and verification, I do not need any of that stuff to make a decision. Highly intuitive here.

It is like I smell the goodness in something and jump! I see the big picture, way down the road and can strategize how to get there from where I am. I am called a 'Quick Start' in the Kolbe system, and I realized the world needs people like me. It needs the bold and fearless to make changes happen.

Eventually, most of the doctors on the board who I was working with took the Kolbe Index and I learned what I had to adjust and to give them what they needed to make decisions. Check it out! No matter what it says, you are needed for your specific driver.

Drivers are your default setting for how you get things done. Priceless! I was a Quick Start surrounded by Fact Finder/Follow Throughs. No wonder I felt alone! **COOPERATIVE**.

Planning ahead for my birthday, I took a GPS DNA test with a company called GPS Originals and now Home DNA. I heard growing up that our ancestors were German, English, Scotts and Irish, like lots of white Americans. By this time in my life, I had heard other hints and began to wonder what else was in my genetic makeup, as some things did not add up.

For one thing, although Mom was a blue-eyed blonde as a child, Dad had black, straight hair, black-brown eyes, and an olive complexion. I asked Mom once, "Why is Dad so dark?" She answered,

"It's the Black Irish." "What in the world does that mean," I wondered, as obviously Mom was finished talking about it.

I wanted to know where my people came from, where their blood came from and anything else I could find out about them.

The test results came December 19, 2016, and I would never be the same. Even though I did not look like it, with my olive skin, brunette hair and brown eyes, the largest part of my heritage is Scandinavian. Now my brother, Adam who was tall, muscular, and square-jawed made sense for this. I read on … Southern France, okay, Basque, what?

What do we know about the Basque? Orkney Islands, Russia, Tuva and 15% Indian from India! What?! Sardinia, no wonder I pine for the Greek Islands! And little bits of all kinds of other things like African, Moroccan, and Middle Eastern. I read through the whole report then sat there. I had given myself such a terrific gift! I gasped in joy and felt connected to people all over the world. "I'm global!" I said to myself!

More research was needed, and yet I could see much of my blood came from marauders. I wondered at the courage of my ancestors to be so different in their surroundings. **COMPASSIONATE**.

CHAPTER 19

VIKINGS, MOORS & TESTS

*It is better to have less thunder in the mouth and
more lightning in the hand.*
—APACHE PROVERB

It seems crazy, yet once again I pulled my natal chart in 2019, like it would be different. At this point, I was grasping at straws, looking for some hope against hope my life could be easier. It is not sad. It simply is what it is. One woman searching for more.

In February of 2020, I did a DISC Style Report still searching for answers. I found the report entirely left-brained and dry. I did not even read the entire thing for months. It claimed I am dominant and get things done. I already knew that about myself! Thanks for the verification!

Later in November of 2020, my daughter, Tegan, recommended I take the Strengths Finder test. You know I'm happy taking tests!

Dad taught me how to take them, and I am good at it! So, bring it on!

I learned I am strategic, creating systems to make things happen. I am a connector, connecting people, places and things and ever learning. I build strong relationships, which also makes things happen. Yup. I knew all that. **WISE**.

Last year, I also got a spontaneous intuitive reading from my daughter's friend. Danica was talking about me, and her friend, Kelly, got intuitive hits for me which were spot on and a nice surprise.

She said it was time to let go of my job, to do what I was destined or designed to do. She said I should look at certain people in my life with new eyes, see them for who they truly are and let go. She was entirely correct. And I should have let go of them way sooner than I did! Not being a quitter is sometimes a curse! Good thing I am open to learning from my decisions. Being teachable is the best definition of humility I know. Be humble, so you can learn! **TEACHABLE**.

HUMBLE.

My GPS DNA report showed migration patterns and gave reasons for them. My people were Vikings, Russians, and Moors, who were all known for conquering weaker people. Basque people are shepherds and gypsies. Even the castes of Indian were basket and weapon makers historically and tended to be scientists and educators now, which is what my father was.

That makes sense for my dad as he was in academia most of his career in addition to running an active practice treating patients. The other caste are also gypsies, so now we have a pattern. No wonder when I get stressed; my tendency is to bolt! I asked my friend who grew up in Pakistan what she knew of these castes. She said, "The one caste are professors, and the other word means 'bastard!'" Well, there ya go! Colorful. I come from colorful people.

It did not take me long to recognize my people likely always had a rough go of it. They probably did not look like others where they lived, and I can only imagine what it might have been like for them. I hoped they had faith in something, which helped them get through whatever life threw at them. I was grateful for the trials of my ancestors and prayed prayers of thanksgiving for the tough people from whence I came. **EMPATHY.**

Park Forest, Illinois is the Chicago suburb where I grew up. It was a singular time in history and a very interesting village. Park Forest was the first totally green-built community of its kind in the world, that I know of. The Smithsonian has an exhibit on it. There are books written about it. The village was designed for GIs coming home from war. One of the things we did not talk about much was the number of grandparents of my school pals who survived the Holocaust.

I heard their stories in their thick accents. I saw the tattooed numbers on their arms. I remember much of it still today. One story sticks out because I want it to.

I remember an older woman smiling while she talked about the music. She said they could not sing their songs, so they had to sing them in their heads, which gave them joy. Joy—in a Nazi concentration camp. Joy, while their family and friends died in front of them. Joy, in the cold and starvation. Joy was a choice, even under the worst of circumstances. It was impressed into my soul. We can choose joy. **HAPPY.**

There are always things for which to be grateful. Always. No matter what I or my kids or my ancestors had been through, we could choose Joy.

You can choose joy, no matter what.

"God will only give you what you would have asked for if you knew everything he knows." Timothy Keller. It is not a bad idea to read this quote again.

My neighbor was talking over the back fence one day about how good my boys were at keeping the yard clean and mowed and getting along. I shared how important it was in our family for everyone to pull their weight, including the first chore my kids get is throwing their tightly wrapped diapers away.

She paused, then said, "Maybe it's time to teach my daughter responsibility."

"How old is she?" I asked, imagining a toddler, and smiling.

"16."

I know I do not have a poker face yet I'm certain I tried to hold one. Holy geez! 16 years old and never learning how to do chores in the household where you live? OMG! It could be entirely too late! **RESPONSIBLE**.

'Train up a child when he is young and when he is old, he will not depart from it,' is in the Bible somewhere. It stuck with me. I could not send my sons out into the world without knowing how to clean up after themselves, do their own laundry without messing up the colors and to generally be of help. My kids' father came from a home where the mother did everything. It is disrespectful to put everything on one busy adult! These guys knew how to plan meals and cook, and they were all good at something in the kitchen. Just like the family I was raised in.

In all my questions that I had asked in the 8 days Jason was in a coma, it never occurred to me to ask if they had induced his coma medically.

I assumed he was in a coma because he was in really bad shape. So now they announce they are taking him off the drugs, keeping him in a coma, and I had a few moments of being pissed off inside, while I processed that information. My right eye is twitching just writing about this story 20 years later! That would have been a good thing to know for my psyche and mental health! I had believed it was up to me to create a scenario which would inspire Jason on some deep level to pop out of his coma and react! Clueless! I was clueless!

Jason came out of his coma after eight days, and it was three days after that he figured out who I was, which was really emotional for him. He grabbed me and held me to his chest hard, not letting me go. He was terrified!

He told me he had been to London and England and that their cartoons were messed up. He said he had witnessed a drug deal gone bad and somebody getting shot and killed and they saw that he saw it and they were after him. He did not want me to leave so I could keep him safe from the bad guys.

We have both since decided that we are allergic to morphine because Jason believes it gave him memories, not hallucinations, but real memories.

Now being someone who has done quite a bit of studying of the quantum realm, I'm not so sure he didn't actually experience what he remembers, somehow. I do know it was very real for him, and I was glad I was there to give him a feeling of safety.

There are a lot more parts to the story, of course, which I may share later. Just know, Jason survived this and other very difficult challenges in his life and has created a life he enjoys in Arizona with his half chihuahua, half German Shepherd dog, Butch.

Right now, he is the only one of my kids who does not live in the same valley in Utah where I live. I make an annual visit to see him and he comes up here to go camping and see his siblings. It will not surprise you that I find any time spent with him at all to be a treasure because I could have lost him so many times in his life.

By the way, later, when we told him about our discussion of his glass eyeball options, he laughed and liked mine best! I smile when I think of him laughing.

CHAPTER 20

FROM MEN TO BOYS TO MEN

Where there is true hospitality, not many words are needed.

—ARAPAHO PROVERB

L iving in a house full of boys, the priority for buying clothes was to buy them to fit the oldest and hand them down. Since I was the only girl for 11 years and then had three little sisters in a row, getting me clothes was not a high priority, ever. **WISE**.

My clothes came from hand-me-downs from the ladies at church. Considering it was the 1960s, strange items of clothing would appear in donation bags to me, looking something like torture devices. I came to find out they were girdles, garter belts and bras, which looked positively horrifying. **TOLERANT**.

I never looked really cool at school, although I do remember a couple of things, I fell in love with at first sight. I had a seersucker summer top and big bouffant skirt with pockets that I loved to wear every Sunday to church. The back of the waistband had to be safety pinned, as it was too big. And even though she was an award-winning fashion designer, I could assume my mother did not take the waistband apart and fit it to me because I was a growing girl. That's the story I tell myself now anyway! **ADULTING**.

One time, a donation bag for our family had a navy-blue button-up-the-front smock with patch pockets in front. I was delighted! I claimed I was an artist, and I wore it over my clothes!

I remember one evening I tossed a bunch of fake flowers across my carpeted bedroom floor. I had no painting supplies, but I did have paper and a pencil to sketch. I do not believe I had any artistic talent along these lines whatsoever, yet wearing the smock, I was an artist! **CREATIVE**.

My mother opened my door when showing our house to a potential buyer saying, "My daughter is an artist," and then closed the door. It warmed my heart that she would play along.

I never understood why adults do what they do. Dad never complimented me on my looks like I heard him when talking about other females. The word he liked to use was "gorgeous." What he did compliment me for was intelligence. I was smart in being able to spell, even words I did not know. I looked for things to learn to impress my dad.

It is a handicap going through life thinking the world revolves around you. I wouldn't know. Growing up in trauma, you won't believe that. I used to believe you cannot have compassion for others unless you have suffered. I may still believe that.

It would be nice if we all were naturally thoughtful, considerate, and nothing happened for us to lose that. Pretty sure it doesn't work like that. Compassion and understanding on a deeper level may require suffering. That combination also may birth empathy, which is truly a higher-level character trait. **EMPATHY**.

I have only witnessed one child who seemingly came wicked as her behavior from a very early age was frightening. Do not know if she had been through some kind of trauma early or not. Yet besides her, all other kids I have known have been sweet and open minded. Life, adults, and choices can knock that innocence out of us.

One of my earliest memories was Mom making me show my father what he did to me. She stayed behind the kitchen wall and sent me into the living room where Dad was waking up on the couch.

I stepped around all the empty beverage containers beside the couch to turn around and lift up the skirt of my little dress.

Large red handprints covered my back. It was years later before I remembered what happened before.

My father grabbed my forearm, lifted me off the ground and with the full force of a grown man, laid into my back with his other hand.

I have no idea what my father may have endured as a child to think on some level that beating a 3-year-old is ever okay.

He also thought it was okay to bandage tape around the ankles and wrists of my little brothers and across their mouths.

Both of my parents felt it was okay to leave them like that on a concrete basement floor, taped around a support pole. Since I was oldest in that house at 8, the oldest my brothers could have been were 4 and 6, likely younger.

Knowing Dad's upbringing, he had to have dealt with betrayal, abandonment and probably abuse of all kinds. These learned behaviors get passed down without intervention. You have to learn there is another way or you believe these behaviors are normal and repeat them.

I did my best to be a perfect child although deception consistently was a presence in our family.

People around us said we had a perfect family, and we smiled, thanking them. From Mom, we learned little white lies were okay. Not to say our parents didn't do a great amount of good. This is about the fact that parents are also growing up while raising their kids, and if they grew up with trauma, they have to recognize it first and then consciously work to improve themselves. If not, generation after generation comes and goes doing the same damn bad habits. **HONEST**.

I loved each of my kids raising them. I did not want to repeat the dark side of how I was raised and yet I did.

When I was pregnant with my 6th baby, we lived in a sketchy old house with electrical wires added as an afterthought. Our heat was provided the same way I was able to cook, on a wood and coal-burning stove in the living room. We did have running cold water, which was a blessing, after having to haul water for the previous two years.

One day I was sweeping the living room, when 9-year-old Trevor came up behind me to tell me something. I spun around with the broom in one hand and hit him on the top of his head with it for no reason at all. None. I was not angry at him or anyone else.

Why in the world I hit him in the head with a broom handle I may never know. It was one of the worst things I've ever done in my life.

I grabbed him, put my hand on his head and quickly got ice on it. I didn't know why I did that and told him so. Apologizing over and over, I made a pact with him and God that I would never do that again. It's a terrible memory. **HUMBLE**.

It got my attention to commit to breaking that family habit of violence with me. I am grateful something shifted significantly for me that day. **TEACHABLE**.

CHAPTER 21

RESILIENCY ALERT

If something can be destroyed
by truth, it should be.

How do you move forward after an experience like Trevor and the broom? Because it really happened. **COURAGE**.

Just because something has always been done one way, does not mean it's right. It does not mean you have to keep doing it that way or doing it at all. You can get to a place where you recognize it's not good enough, so you look for a better option.

Also, just because you believe something, does not make it true. I question everything and taught my kids to do so, too. That's how I live my whole life. I saw so many problems growing up in my parent's household. This book touches on a few.

Then, I saw so many problems in my own marriage and the family we created. Just like my parents and just like his parents, the two of us had brought all kinds of bad habits into our household. Like the story of my son, Trevor, and I, when he was a kid and I hit him with the broom, there were many things which really needed to be stopped, done away with, or corrected in some way. **ADULTING**.

The same can probably be said for you in your life. Has this book helped you see things in your old life just as wonky, wacky, or incorrect as my life? Even one thing you can mindfully fix?

This is when you get to look at it hard and decide if it's correct. You can choose a whole new life, one day at a time. I am NOT the only person who has done this. Sharing my stories is intended to help you see that if I can do it, with so much stacked against me, so can you. Or someone in your life who needs this can be helped, too.

Being resilient in the face of life's challenges is not easy and yet it's really the only healthy way to navigate your way through. People react in all kinds of ways when they do not get their way. They yell, get violent, blame someone else, lie, get passive/aggressive and default to other unacceptable behaviors. I picture a temper tantrum adult as a little kid who never learned a better way to behave.

And I swear there are adults who never grew up past their childhood temper tantrums. Haven't you seen adults do the craziest things like they just reverted to a 3 or 13-year-old? I surely have!

I saw a grown man throw himself forward from the waist exclaiming, "why?" when he did not get his way! He was asked to have a conversation that he did not want to have. It was as if he regressed to a three-year-old in an instant.

I see adults cave in to lying and/or the blame game when they have done something out of line. It is also crazy to see in business, yet it happens. Instead of taking responsibility and looking for a solution, they simply affix the blame elsewhere, which is a very cheap, immature, and deceptive behavior to have in business.

This is a good time to look hard at ourselves. Which of our poor habits, no longer serving us, can we let go of? And by 'we' I mean you! I am working on this for myself all the damn time! And what good character traits can we develop in their stead? I do this all the damn time as well.

Every time someone else's behavior gets my attention, I immediately ask myself, "Do I do that?" Because it is repulsive, and that is not how I intend to go through life. My daily intention is to make a positive difference. Changing poor behaviors is not something to put off. It is not good for us or anyone around us. **SPIRITUAL**.

If we looked like our character, would we be lovely or hideous or something in the middle?

Instead of procrastinating when we do not want to do something, we can use Mel Robbin's technique of counting down from five and then jumping into action. You don't wanna get out of bed? Count 5, 4, 3, 2, 1 and jump out of bed. Make that new habit instead of procrastinating and see how different your life becomes.

Oh, ya know, it can be that easy. Normally, people think changes take time. Picture an XY graph with zero at the axis point. Over time and exerted effort, people can change, improving, with setbacks, yet still moving forward. Or you can just decide differently and jump! Nearly straight up on the XY graph! Life as you know it has changed, and new opportunities come your way.

This story may sound out of date and yet it is what I did as a kid. I do not know how old I was at the time, 12? Maybe 13? Somewhere in there is when I figured out what sex was.

Now Dad had explained it to me when I was about 9 or 10. We were in the family car together, and for some reason, he must have felt it was time to give me the 'talk' about developing as a girl to a woman. We were on the way to a professional function, and I was all dressed up in a fancy bouffant skirted party dress, and my hair was actually brushed.

I leaned forward in the back seat to hear what he was saying. Something about words I did not know and how stuff was going to come out of me someday and not to worry about it. "It is healthy and normal," he said. I was thinking it sounded horrifying and inconvenient and I asked him, "Why?"

"This is how your body works so you can have a baby someday. Or lots of babies in your life," he explained.

"How does that work?" I asked. Geez. If I had known what would come next, I never would have asked, preferring to wallow in my childhood ignorance.

"A man puts his penis in a woman's vagina to make babies," Dad explained to my question.

Why I could not help myself is beyond me, looking back, and yet I commented, "Gross! Why would they do that?" I asked. Sheesh.

"It feels good," Dad said.

"Aaaaack, gross!" I responded. I must have been such a fun kid to have around!

Even though this gross conversation was burned into my young brain, I put it out of my mind and did not think about it again until the wise old age of about 13. My Sunday School teacher was talking about staying pure and not having sex until we were married. Made sense to me as I still thought it was gross. I made the conscious decision right then to never have sex until I was married. I made this decision once and never had to make it again. **BOUNDARIED.**

Situations and opportunities came up and I extracted myself from them. I set a goal and expected boys, guys, and men to respect it. If they did not, I did not want them in my life. This was too important to me.

You can do this with anything. I believe it is one of the great ways addicts manage addiction. They say, "Enough." "Basta." And one day at a time, they stick to their new life until they can celebrate 1 day sober. 1 week sober. 1 month and you get it. Even something as tough as addiction can be handled when you just decide. **COURAGE**.

CHAPTER 22

THE HAPPY LIST

Many hands make work light;
many ideas open the way.
—HMONG PROVERB

Now, if I could focus on just one project to completion. That would be neat!

"Lol, maybe you just need a full day of relaxation and quiet, and the projects can start tomorrow," my daughter-in-law Lizz wrote.

Well, I hand watered outside since they turned the auxiliary water off in the neighborhood.

I swept and mopped the whole main floor. Unpacked decorations from last week's event. Switched laundry over then folded, hung up and put it all away. Started a cork board project. Ran out of corks, so it can just dry now. Read a digital book on marketing. Made some connections on social media while screwing around online. Handled some finance shizz. Built a spreadsheet for last weekend's event and added the information from 60 business cards. Drafted an email with four versions and sent them out.

Then I can call it good. It was 8:36 a.m. on a Monday.

Someone told me I do more before 9 a.m. than most people do in a week! That's funny! I have my fingers in too many pies, as I do not know which one will benefit me the most, or if any will. That is the stress. Too much to think about.

My roommate/son-in-law, Jason told me to just take it easy while they are gone. I just laughed. House to myself and I think deep clean. Thanks, Mom. She instilled that in me over every spring break as a kid. Other families took vacations somewhere warm. We cleaned. Now I'm rambling ... What do I need to do next?

Having a limiting belief, 'I have no value unless I am producing something in the moment' is hard on the soul. One of the ways I have worked on that one is to convince myself I have intrinsic worth. Another method is to tell myself that relaxing and breathing have tremendous value.

It has taken eons of time to let myself stop and walk away from what I am doing to regroup. I need to go pee right now and yet I am still editing this book and know if I walk away, I will be done for the night. It is 8:44 p.m. Go ahead and laugh. You do it, too.

I have a collection of things I can do to rejuvenate and clear the stress and cobwebs from my mind. My purpose is to get back to what I was doing, I confess, so it has not taken complete hold of me. It has become obvious to me that when I walk away from projects to get recentered, I am much better at accomplishing things quickly. I can sit in the sun, let my mind wander and answers or solutions come. **CALM**.

This story falls into the make lemonade out of lemons even in small things category.

My brain was fried after working in front of a laptop for hours. I went into the kitchen for a frosty beverage. Then I noticed things needing attention.

So, I was just trying to straighten up the kitchen a little bit and stocking a case of coconut LaCroix in the pantry. One of the cans fell out of the carton, hitting the floor, poking a hole in the side of the can.

Cold sparkling coconut-scented water sprayed everywhere! My entire body, head to toe got sprayed, along with the stove, the fridge, the counter, all around the coffee pot and of course, the floor between the can and all of those items. I laughed at the disaster and grabbed the mop.

The whole kitchen now required a mopping, so pretty much the whole floor is mopped now! Looks impressive! Lemonade out of lemons, even in small (sticky) things. And now I am relaxed again and can get back to it. I think, "Thank you, Jesus!" **HAPPY**.

Even in little things, we can find relief. Years ago, some friends and I started a Happy List on Facebook.

Note: Facebook in its infinite wisdom has since deleted the 'Notes' section from my profile with zero warning. #Asshats. I had treasures in there! Personal recipes I shared. Notes from books I read, like my own version of Cliff Notes. And the famous Happy List.

Many friends added to it over the years. Perhaps I should try it again. See what it would look like now.

The original Happy List was things we could do or think about to snap out of bad moods or get through a tough time. Included on the list were things like butterflies, fireworks, all kinds of flowers with descriptions of colors and scents, types of pets, smelling yummy things like a new baby's neck, lilacs, and the rain. Three of my favorites! There were things like reconnecting with school chums, kissing and getting a really big hug. Not everything on the list would work for whatever ailed you.

If you were suffering from a breakup, hugging, and kissing weren't things to think about. If your parent just died and you were empty after the funeral, me going off about how yummy carnations smell would not help you since they seem to fill funeral bouquets.

There was one thing on the list we all agreed would not offend us no matter what we were going through as it is ridiculous and always made us snort. We put it on the top of the list and to this day, it is also a salutation when some of us talk to each other. **COOPERATIVE.**

HAPPY LIST:

1. **WASABI PEAS**. Wasabi peas are so ridiculous to think about and to say, they tend to snap us out of it for a moment, snicker, giggle, or snort and relax our shoulders for a moment! Try it!

WASABI PEAS.

See? Ridiculous!

Humor is one of the most important components of navigating crappy things in life although some people have trouble with it. They believe laughter at a funeral is disrespectful. When things go wrong during a wedding, and they always do, we are supposed to hold our laughter in. Poppycock. Laughter is a great relaxer. Laughter is a great connector. Laughter can start the healing process. I am a big fan of letting laughter rip and letting the consequences fall where they may. **HUMOR.**

Dad told the story of one of his patients which explains this concept very well. Way back in the day, patients wore treating gowns wherein they took off their clothes, put on a patient gown with ties in the back. This was so doctors could look at the spine they were examining and check a patient's gait and such to see what was going on with them. During examination, patients would have to bend side to side and frontwards and backwards to measure range of motion.

One day, Dad was examining a new patient. She was wearing her patient gown yet had not tied the back ties very well. When she bent forward to see that range of motion of touching her toes or whatnot, two things happened at the same time and her response struck my dad as hilarious!

She bent forward and her gown fell to the floor, so she was naked AND her wig fell off AND rolled out of reach. She stepped over the gown to grab her wig, shoving it back on her head, and only then did she think to grab her gown to cover herself.

Dad maintained his composure when both items fell off, but when she grabbed the wig first, he lost it and started laughing. He excused himself, and she dressed and left, mortified.

Man, to be able to have things like this happen to you and laugh at the absurdity is a great skill and habit to develop. It makes it harder for jerks to make fun of you, if you really do not care what others think. If you can feel strong enough on the inside, those circumstances do not rattle you. You can handle tough times much better. **ADAPTABLE**.

Also, if you can have a ready kind word and gentle actions to calm others, you are a hero. When people can trust your discretion with their vulnerability that is noble. You can do this. You can develop the strength and peace of mind to handle the tough moments with resiliency. And if you really have to tell somebody, tell me. I probably won't share. **COMPASSIONATE**.

Start your own Happy List. Write down things which make you happy, sometimes, all the time, once in a while. You will be surprised how long you can make this list! I started my Happy List in the back of my Gratitude Journal in hopes they would collide in the middle somewhere. Do it! You will be happy you did!

CHAPTER 23

SHOW ME DAUGHTER

*The caribou feeds the wolf, but it is the wolf who
keeps the caribou strong.*

—INUIT PROVERB

This past year and a half, as it may have been for you, has
been the most difficult year of my life. It has been unrelent-
ingly painful and as strong and resilient as I am, I have cried
out for relief!

My trust has been shaken. My faith has been tried. Brain fog has
been a thing when the stresses of my life have gotten to me. I have
refused to use the word 'overwhelm' as I do not choose to identify
as weak any more. I have drawn on my heritage of resilient parents
and ancestors. I have become my mother's "Show Me" daughter.
I have been my father's continually learning daughter. (Dad got
another doctorate in his 70s in philosophy!) I have put all my tools

to use and am still standing. Strong. Capable. Resilient. Through what, you ask?

In a nutshell, on top of everything else that is challenging in my life, just being the mother of nine children, with nine relationships with spouses and partners, and 15 grandkids is a lot of people to care about. And with my 10 siblings and their families, that is a lot of human beings to be involved with and care about!

Then, in my job I was responsible for over 1,000 doctors in Utah and there were so many complicated challenges with that position, my life was mostly on the edge some days. In a short period of time, too many things were piled on me on top of everything else.

I had excruciating changes in my job, which were unfair and un-necessary, yet I still had to deal with it. This personally affected me, including cutting my income by a third and taking the rap for something I did not do because I was the Executive Director, and somebody had to be the scapegoat. I felt like I had been cheated on, ganged up on and hung out to dry.

So, I had to move across the valley to Herriman, Utah, near the Kennecott Copper Mine, which is visible from space apparently. I might as well have moved to East Nevada! I know this was a bless-ing but a hard one because, I love living alone and having all my beautiful things around and an income. I thought back to raising kids when nothing stayed where I put it, and people were messy, and I did not want that again. It is a trigger and I knew it. I liked my simple, quiet life after the chaos of most of it! I missed a simple, clean life, growing hundreds of flowers every year.

Then, my younger brother, Adam, died with no warning. As the oldest of 11 siblings, I had never lost a sibling before.

Then, two people very dear to me lost their children over Christ-mas that year. I cannot imagine the heartbreak. So, I prayed for and with them.

In the spring, I went to Chicago to help my sister-in-law handle things she was challenged with after the death of her husband.

I came back to Utah for a board meeting, expecting to get a two-months retainer, which is how I was paid, plus a $4,000 or $5,000 bonus for my extraordinary efforts of the last two pandemic years.

Personally, two years previously, I had applied for a mortgage to finally get my own place, which I have never had in my life only to be told I was denied because I did not make enough money to own a home. That had been devastating, but I had been saving money for a down payment and anticipated having a chunk of cash to add to it after this board meeting.

That last year had been such a hard job with so many complications, yet I had done it and saved the association so much money in the process, that I had expected to be rewarded. This, in a year in which I did twice as much work as I had done in the previous three years because of Covid and still having to be in compliance and provide continuing education for the doctors online without the correct systems and those trials of all of this work just went on and on.

Instead, the board opted to not renew my contract for the next year, so I did not get one dime.

They dangled the carrot of a $5,000 bonus if I would, in eight days, on top of still doing my job, also complete an enormous list of tasks to prepare whoever was taking over my job. It was also a condition to sign a letter of non-disparagement that I would not talk about my job with anybody, ever, for eternity, to receive the aforementioned bonus.

I sent the letter of non-disparagement to my attorney, and he told me give them all of their belongings back, to not complete the extra tasks and let them keep their bonus.

I also asked my dear friend, Dennis, who had retired from a corporate position, for his recommendation. His countenance shifted when I told him what they were asking of me, and he also told me to walk away and let them go. He told me not to do what they had asked for, as it was completely unreasonable. That was my last personal conversation with Dennis. And I will never forget his kindness to me.

I walked away from the passion I had put into that position and two months later, our dear friend, Dennis, his wife, Sandy, and our friend, Heidi and I all got the Corona virus, which knocked me on my butt for over a month. It took all my energy away for a month, and even though I knew my friends were sick, I did not know what was going to happen to Dennis, who was hospitalized. It was such a situation of helplessness that I knew was all in God's hands.

In the same month when I was feeling very low, another younger brother, Mark, died and all my siblings were going to his funeral in Missouri and I told them, "I cannot schlepp luggage through the horribly designed Salt Lake airport." I did not have enough energy for that. In the meantime, my baby sister and her family got Covid, so they couldn't come to the funeral either. And my sister, Val, said that she would push me through the airport in a wheelchair because everybody who could be at Mark's funeral should be there.

We were still seriously suffering from the loss of Adam and to lose another brother in less than a year was very painful to us. We felt strongly about holding each other closer. Looking back after this length of time, I have really had to use my strong character traits to navigate this part of my life's journey.

Then later in August 2021, Dennis passed away, too. Another tremendous loss to our community and a personal loss to me.

In fall it had been one year since I lost my younger brother, Adam, and by November 23, I could not put off total knee replacement surgery any longer so even though I was still weak, I did not have a job demanding my time, so I went ahead and got it done. It took me months to recover to the point where I had energy again and other than times when I think I can run up and down 1 million stairs and haul stuff in and out of my car and to different buildings and stand on concrete for hours, I'm doing pretty well!

Eventually, I adjusted somewhat to living with my daughter and her family, after having my own place for so long. They have a lovely home, even if I still am drawn to having my own place. I have appreciated how quiet this little town is without traffic and siren noise, and I have yet to see anything weird here, like what is normal in a bigger city like Salt Lake.

The money I saved for a down payment on my home is what I paid my rent, car payment and all the things with and when that ran out, I had to pull money out of the crypto I had been saving and investing in for some time. There are a couple of programs I was already in to help with my finances. I will share their contact information in the Resource Pages in the back of this book.

One resource I highly recommend is Student Loan Tutor, which, for a small sum, you can hire them to handle your student loan debt. They are trained to navigate all your options so added to your personal situation they make recommendations of a plan moving forward which makes that situation manageable financially. Another resource is 101 Financial where I have a coach who helped me get all of my finances in one spot. This was not hard since I have been using spreadsheets since about 2014 to keep track of outgoing expenses and income.

This particular program set me up to pay off my debt using interest I am no longer paying. You might want to go back and read that sentence again because that's a challenging concept, yet it is absolutely true! And their online program allows me to see a projection for 12 months out of what my finances will look like if nothing changes. That is extremely valuable! On my trajectory currently, without an income, I could be $60,000 in debt if I am not careful! That is probably an exaggeration, but you get my point. The trajectory I was on when I was still working for the association was much more hopeful as you might imagine.

Now I am just hoping people see value in my efforts of putting this book together over the course of a year, and actually a couple of more books which are in the works, to make this a series, and they will pick up a book or two. One to read and one to share with somebody they care about. Now I want to share something else highly impactful to me, which has helped me tremendously to get through this horribly hard year. And that is going to be the focus of this last chapter.

CHAPTER 24

WELL HELL

*Do not judge your neighbor until you walk two
moons in his moccasins.*
—CHEYENNE

I am just grateful to the brim and overflowing! The last couple
of months have definitely made such a dramatic shift in my life
with something to do which makes a difference! I have to be
doing something of purpose for my soul or I feel adrift.

Writing this book has gotten to me more than once, where I had to
stop for a while to regroup. So much harshness, with unrelenting
circumstances, crisis on top of crisis has been nearly impossible to
navigate alone. And yet I was not alone spiritually.

My daughter, Tegan, invited me to a Thanksgiving service at a
church she had started attending a few years ago. I had zero interest in organized religion after my experiences in my childhood

church. Stories for another book, perhaps. Yet I love holidays and went with her.

The service was lovely, gracious and I sat there thinking, "I'm not offended by anything here, yet."

Periodically, she had asked me if I wanted to join her and Matthew, her son, my grandson, and sometimes I went. Once I was dropping them off, wearing an old baggy University of Utah sweatshirt, ripped jeans, and river sandals. My plan was to hike about Red Butte Gardens above the university until it was time to pick them up. She asked if I wanted to come in, and I exclaimed, "look at how I'm dressed!"

"No one will care," she assured me. I thought, "we'll see about that" and went in the church. She was right, no one cared how I was dressed.

Eventually, I started going because I wanted to. And making a new friend helped.

Tegan invited me, my younger daughter, Danica, and my daughter-in-law, Mary, to a women's gathering to make Christmas ornaments and wreaths. I walked in the south doors and a woman standing at the north doors raised her voice to say, "You're Roxy! Tegan's mom! Get over here!"

To which I responded, "You're not the boss of me!" as I walked over to her. That was the beginning of a beautiful friendship with Sandy. She asked me to sit with her in the early morning meetings on Sunday and I started going to Capital Church in Salt Lake City every week. I am not alone in being welcomed by Sandy, and I call it being Sandyfied!

Even with my strong opinions of religion and hypocritical religious people, I came to Capital Church finding nothing like that there among those people. The intent is to live a Christ-centered life of truly caring about others, because it is the correct thing to do, not for any gain.

Every week's message comes from our down-to-earth pastor, Troy, with his quirky sense of humor, which has inspired and motivated me to be a better version of myself during the coming week. There was no pressure. No judgment. No looking down at others. No elitist behavior anywhere. What the founders, Troy, and Suzanne Champ, had intended was what they had created and when I was ready for them, they were ready for me.

Now, in a critically challenging time in our nation and world, I have belonging in community, which I have never felt before. People care about me and my struggles in very healing ways. Gentle, gracious, and just what I needed. And even better, they have various ways I can be helpful, too. Odds are good, if you show up one Sunday, I might be hosting at one of the doors, welcoming you and smiling so you feel welcome.

We need community which feels like this. I truly hope you find a place and a people where you feel like I do being part of the Capital Community.

I have looked over my life considering how to make it better for the rest of it. What have I learned and what do I still need to learn? Raising my kids was monumental and not for the faint of heart. Yet my life is not yet over, so what else can I do?

I have shared much of my story about my oldest son's coma and how it affected me and what I learned. I have talked a bit about my marriage and it's ending and other stories here and there in my life. My hope is you saw yourself in there somewhere and do not feel so alone. My saga continues yet we can wrap up what you have read so far in this chapter.

Back to the story I mentioned in the Introduction to this book of what happened to Trevor and my genius idea for fixing it.

He was 6 years old when his brother came running in the house to get a parent. Not good. If Trevor could not blast into the house with a tale of horror, something is terribly wrong. **CALM**.

Even though I was pregnant with son #5, I waddled quickly out to the paddock, beside the house we were renting at the time.

Trevor was sitting in the middle of the paddock holding his foot. As I got closer, I could not figure out what I was looking at. FYI: this is a theme when you have sons.

A rusty old hanger, whose hook part was flattened to itself, was sticking through the bottom of Trevor's foot, and I could see it pushing the top of his foot's skin up. Geez. Boys. Before doing anything, I paused to consider what I knew. **CALM**.

He was in a horse corral, sitting in dried manure, with an old rusty double-width hanger causing a puncture wound. Well, there ya go. All the factors for tetanus in one spot. Nice, Trevor. Before either his father or I could go off on why he was even in the paddock without an adult, I said, "Carry him and his new attachment into the house, so I can call my midwife. She will know what to do."

When I got my midwife on the phone, she rattled off a list of odd-named herbs of which I had no idea what she was talking about. She quickly figured that out and slowed down to explain a few things. I did have a small pot of calendula salve I had purchased from her, so she told me to get it.

"Should I wash his foot off first I asked?"

"That is the least of your worries," she said. "Boys and their sports will get them into more scrapes than you can imagine."

She did not know I had 7 brothers and was going on my fifth son.

On the phone, she directed me to smooth calendula salve on the skin around the wound as soon as I removed the hanger from his foot. "Pull the hanger straight out," she said. "Now, wrap his foot with gauze. This will give the gunk inside a place to go when it comes out."

I'm wondering how gunk is going to get out of there and if I should squeeze it like a zit. I do not squeeze it as my second thought because that was dumb. **COURAGE**.

Instead of using any of the plethora of herbs she had mentioned before, she told me to grate a root vegetable like an onion, carrot, or potato as they are built to draw liquid and nutrients from their surroundings. That made sense.

So, I grated an onion, a carrot, and a potato for good measure. I really did not know what I was doing. I was running on pure faith and trust. Faith in my knowing to call my midwife was intuition from God and trust that she knew what she was doing after all her years. **SPIRITUAL**.

The whole onion, carrot, and potato were lumped together under Trevor's foot. Then, I slipped a bread sack over the mess and wrapped an Ace bandage around everything so it would stay on all night, as she directed. Thinking about this now, it never occurred to me a 6-year-old would mess with it or take it off in the night, yet now, experienced me would know that!

All night long, I fretted and worried. I did go into Trevor's room to check on him. I just kept praying I had done the right thing and that he would be better in the morning. It was so hard. These are the things which should have given me silver hair much younger in life.

Should I have taken him to a doctor? Would this old-fashioned method work? Was he going to get lockjaw? Was I a bad mom?

Fortunately for all of us, Trevor left the thing alone all night and slept fine with it attached. I picked him up, setting him on the kitchen counter. I wanted to see this up close and personal.

I peeled off the Ace bandage. Then, I carefully pulled the bread sack with icky vegetables and cleaned up the bits which had spilled onto the countertop. Then, I took a deep breath and peeled off the gauze. Holy crap!

The gauze bandage side next to his foot had a big rusty-colored circle in the middle! It had worked!

Holy crap! I was so relieved! It really worked! I called to tell my midwife. I wish I could remember her name. It will come to me eventually, and I'll put it in a later book. Oh it's Jeanne!

In the meantime, she had no doubt. She asked which vegetable I had used.

"All of them," I answered. "Ah ha ha ha ha ha," she nearly cackled. "You didn't need them all!" **HUMOR**.

Well, whatever. It worked! I felt empowered and ready to learn more. What else did I not know which could benefit my growing family? What else would help me be more resilient to the continuous challenges I faced? Only time would tell, as I pressed ahead on my journey of rounding the curves of my bizarre life. **PERSEVERANCE**.

HAPPY LIST

Things I am grateful for and make me or my friends happy:

- Number one - paper clips
- Safety pins
- Zippers
- Buttons

(I saw I was making a list of things which hold stuff together. The irony was not lost on me! At a time when I could not hold my life together!) **HUMOR**.

- My pillow
- My bed
- The fact that I could go to a farmers' market and for four dollars get a big bunch of ranunculi to bring color into my home.
- Once a week I could go to the Hawaiian store and buy one lily, or one tuber rose which would make my entire home smell like heaven.
- My two tall wood backed olive green suede stools at my counter, which I found through Craigs List. I had to drive through the Santa Cruz mountains to pick them up and my friend Dave helped me. I still have them, and they and their memories make me smile.
- Friends of all kinds. (That was not cheating because it was just a group not one individual.)
- Standing on East Cliff and feeling the negative ions from waves of the Monterey Bay lapping on the shore.Doors with locks.
- My Toyota Tundra which has doors with locks. And windows and a corrugated bedliner so I can haul things without damaging them and how much I love driving my truck and how

handy it has been for me in my life. It had suicide doors… so cool…

- My willingness to make substantial changes in life including moving across the country from Ogden, Utah to Santa Cruz, California. Or later from Eugene OR back to Salt Lake City, my second hometown.
- Being able to hear the surf while lying in my bed.
- My kids are resourceful and enterprising, creating their own independent lives.
- My pretty mango-colored dishes.
- My pretty hand-painted wine glasses.
- The daily farmers market in Capitola, which is open year-round, having low prices on all kinds of produce, seeds, nuts, and things I love to eat. (I am back to farmers markets!)
- Being able to eat healthy foods, easily and affordably, where I live.
- My ash gray Toms.
- The parts of my body which are healthy, pain-free, and strong.
- Very cool people I keep meeting in my life. I can learn from their experiences, things I would not normally see.
- Avocado soup. Okay most any soup, stew or chili. It's my bohemian heart or habit from cooking for a big family.
- Breeze in my hair
- Hoodies to keep me warm when I'm letting the breeze blow in my hair.
- I recognize I don't speed when driving anymore. I believe it's because I'm where I want to be.
- Paddle boarding in the harbor alone or with a friend or family member.
- Locally owned restaurants.
- Locally owned coffee shops.
- Having skills, I can use to bless others' lives. **COMPASSIONATE**.

- Giving gifts for no reason.

- Realizing I don't need to swear as I have an extensive vocabulary and I'm smart enough to use it correctly.

- Cotton on my skin

- Linen on my skin

- Having a vehicle with a tailgate I can back onto the beach and drop to sit on and watch the surf. And the birds. And people. And smoke a clove. And drink alkaline water in my water bottle with a Peace symbol on it and be totally in the moment in nature.

- Having gifts from people reminding me I am loved when they are not around.

- Time spent with grandchildren. Any time at all spent with grandkids! Hugs, smiles, holding a little one on my lap. Telling them stories.

- Being with my children and or their partners

- Facing the sun and feeling its warmth on my face

- Wiggling my toes into warm sand until they reach the cold damp sand underneath. **PLAYFUL**.

- Being near running water like rivers and streams

- Listening to the breeze in the tree leaves

- Learning something new

- Blending paint colors

- Seeing another human who smiles when seeing me

- Expressing myself in words

- Listening to music

- Meals with Kim

- Watching plants grow and flowers bloom.

- Sticking my nose in the scented flower or the neck of a baby or a yummy smelling man.

- Holding hands while walking and talking.

- Snuggling into my man on the couch.

- Watching a baseball game in the summertime with friends and family, with a beer in one hand and a Chicago dog in the other!

- The joy of seeing colors I like! A sleek metallic paint job on a sweet car. Lovely, imported fabric. Polished wood grain.

- Lilacs in bloom. Or hyacinths, or alyssum or sweet William or peonies…

- Watching perennials dance in the breeze like California poppies, bachelor buttons or cosmos.

- Time spent in a stationary store. Or a greenhouse. Or a fabric shop. Or a craft store. Anywhere I can touch the things which interest me!

- Meeting Chicago Cubs fans in public! "Go cubbies!"

RESOURCES

I highly recommend any person, place, or thing in these pages because they helped me. So, I believe they may help you! Check them out and follow up when you get the urge. If you have major student loan debt, DON'T wait! That one will change your life for the better!

TO A PEACEABLE LIFE, *Roxy's blog.*
https://roxycross.wordpress.com/

DAVID BAYER, *Mind Hack Coach.*
https://davidbayer.com/

DR BRENÉ BROWN, *Keeping it awkward, brave, and kind.*
https://brenebrown.com/. *My first introduction to her:*
https://brenebrown.com/videos/ted-talk-the-power-of-vulnerability/

PIPER RUIZ, *Amazing business coach.*
piperruiz.com

WAYNE DYER, *Change Your Thoughts—Change Your Life.*
https://www.drwaynedyer.com/

LOUISE HAY, *You Can Heal Your Life.*
https://www.louisehay.com/

KIMBERLEY ERRIGO, *Transformational Coach and Retreats.*
https://kimberlyerrigo.com/

MEL ROBBINS, *5, 4, 3, 2, 1, Jump!*
https://www.melrobbins.com/

101 FINANCIAL, *Genius program to help you see and handle your finances.*
https://101financial.com/

STUDENT LOAN TUTOR, *If you have student loans call these guys! You won't believe the difference.*
https://www.studentloantutor.com/

HOMEDNA, *One of the best things I've done for myself! Find out who your people really were.*
https://homedna.com/

MYERS-BRIGGS, *discover your personality test for greater understanding of who you are.*
https://www.myersbriggs.org/

KOLBE INDEX. *This cool test shows you your driver. What drives you from within?*
https://kolbe.com/

CLIFTONSTRENGTHS ASSESSMENT, *what are you truly good at which you could be doing for a happier more fulfilling life?*
https://www.gallup.com/cliftonstrengths

DISC PROFILE, *is designed to help people communicate better with greater understanding.*
https://www.discprofile.com/

AL ANON, *a 12-step program for family and friends of alcoholics and actually addicts, too. Highly recommend going to 6 meetings to see how it feels for you.*
https://al-anon.org/al-anon-meetings/

ELIZABETH GILBERT, *who inspired me to look deeply into my life and change it. Big Magic, Eat Pray Love, Committed,*
elizabethgilbert.com

FRY SAUCE RECIPE:

- 2 Mayonnaise/Miracle Whip/Veganaiese
- 1 Ketchup
- Mix 2 to 1, mayo to ketchup.

Make it fancy:

Add any or all of the following: Worcestershire Sauce, Pickle Brine, Paprika, Cayenne, Spices like: Black pepper, garlic powder or garlic salt, Tabasco sauce, hot sauce or some red pepper flakes, apple cider vinegar, lemon juice or even horseradish.

ACKNOWLEDGMENTS

As I sit down to write I am well aware of the sheer volume of influences I've had in my life. Daunting to write them down! My sister, *Val*, recommended I simply use initials! VSZ. Those are hers. One down.

Reading this book, you will get the sense I have a ginormous family. It's true. I'm one of eleven siblings and I had nine kids of my own. As of this writing I also have 15 grandchildren and one great grandson, whom I got to meet once. Regardless of how often I see each of them, I love them all very much and thank them for the wonderful and terrifying, and everything in between, I've been through, because of them. This book is the first of many chronicling those sagas.

Their versions of the stories I share involving us, may differ from mine. That has to do with perspective not validity. I am grateful for all of my ten siblings whom I introduce as my big brothers and big sisters, not because I am the baby of this family, but solely due to my stature. Freaking giants. Mom smoked during her first pregnancy with me... Mom and Dad are both gone and as human as they were, I believe they did the best they could with what they had to work with, which included 11 feral children.

Now my own children, who are all girls except 7...

Jason, for whom I dedicate this book and you'll see why reading on,

Trevor, good Lord, that guy, genius who keeps going against all odds,

David, who is beloved like his name means,

Stephan, who makes me smile and shake my head just thinking about him,

Alex, smack in the middle blazing his own remarkable trail,

Tegan, my beautiful, oldest daughter, and mother of Matthew who calls me his best friend... so far,

Josh, who makes me laugh out loud thinking of his world travels, adventures, and impact,

Connor, my son the Yeti, minding his own beeswax as he cares for family, career, and his truck, of which I'm slightly jealous, and

Danica, an old soul whose friendship and love I could not have navigated this life without. OK, now I'm in tears!

So much love and gratitude for these amazing humans and our combined lives together! Then their spouses/partners, kids etc. and I could write a book just about each of them; the greatest joy in that, is how much reading that last sentence will freak them out. Stay tuned...

Next, friends, mentors, coaches, sponsors, counselors, supporters, authors, and inspirations in my life... Many wearing more than one of those hats. To the benevolent, caring, generous, supportive, honest, loving friends through the years who have been there for me through thick and thin, neither of which sounds attractive to me, I give my heart with the intention of the greatest blessings life has to offer. To *Valerie Cross Valentino*, my non-biological sister, and *Kathy Wursten*, *Jodie Adams*, and *Sandy Pfaff*, with the same title, we have been through unimaginable trials to still be loving and caring women. To *Richard Scheid*, who knows me better than most people and once said, "if your children hadn't had you, they would have had nobody," I honor our meeting in coffee shops hither and yon low these many decades. To *Kimberly Errigo*, *Clint Nelson*, *Kori Johnson*, *Corey*, *Katie*, *Diane*, *Alicia*, and also *Kim*, who I adopted as an older brother I never had, and so many others who were there when I was in greatest need, and would be again should I reach out, my deepest gratitude.

Thanks to my publisher, *Lil*, whose tenacity made me write the book others have asked me for, for years! I am happy to introduce her to aspiring authors as Lil is a gem to work with on these projects!

To *Piper Ruiz* who's spent countless hours encouraging me, sending me clients to help and never wavering in her genuine support, may the heavens open to pour out gifts. To my unnamed friends, chillax. There will be other books with dedications and acknowledgements, and I am thankful you were impressed with my tenacity, generosity, love, and selflessness, urging me to keep going to build this strong character of mine.

My gratitude also goes out to *Troy and Suzanne Champ* who bravely started Capital Church in Salt Lake City, Utah, eons ago and whose staff, family, friends, and congregation welcomed me in when I poked my head in their doors, loved me, set beautiful examples for me, and have yet to offend me.

To the authors of well over 10,000 books I've read, thank you for endless hours of study to learn how to become the best version of myself, all about the world, in and above it, and to simply escape, carry on. Thank you, *Dr Brené Brown*, in particular, for your example of living what you preach and introducing me to *Anne Lamott* whose quote in *Bird by Bird* gave me permission to write about people who did me wrong, even if they weren't dead yet. And to *Elizabeth Gilbert* who inspired me to travel, let people, places, ideas and things go, and to do things half assed to get them done, Danke mucho and hopefully you will not find this book half-assed.

Finally, speaking of half-assed, I would like to thank, yet not encourage, those in my life, either in ignorance, by nature or purposefully, who have unapologetically made my life and the lives of people I loved harder, once, or consistently. It is you who have provided the life experiences for me to learn the harder, soul crushing lessons in life which have made me the most resilient person my youngest daughter knows and admires. It is you who, without fail, inspired me to dig deep within, work harder against all odds, to persevere, which inspired my publisher to pick me out of a workshop full of successful entrepreneurs, to write this book about resiliency and how to get it. I am grateful for the opportunity to become the incredibly solid champion and ally to underdogs everywhere, and to be able to round the curves of my life with grace and aplomb. Unfortunately for your souls, you are still negative, destructive narcissists. #asshats.

To everyone else, namaste and welcome to the Resiliency Party wherein you can learn to navigate whatever life throws your way! Grace and peace!

ROXY CROSS has a great love for children, believing motherhood is a sacred honor with great responsibility. Oldest of 11, Roxy had nine children of her own, has 15 grandchildren and one great grandson, so far. Being highly intuitive, she enjoys making jewelry, painting abstracts, and designing fabulous flower baskets growing food plants in with flowers. Roxy lives in Salt Lake Valley near her children and grandkids enjoying the grandeur of being surround-ed by mountains with occasional road trips and flights to see the rest of the world.

www.ingramcontent.com/pod-product-compliance
Lightning Source LLC
Chambersburg PA
CBHW052020030426
42335CB00026B/3219